Prais
Childre

"Using practical strategies and relatable language, Bridgett Miller shows parents how to help their children reach their potential while keeping their own inherent joy and peace intact. Our children will be more content and capable as a result of us taking in the wisdom of *What Young Children Need You to Know*—and so will we."

Rachel Macy Stafford *New York Times*–bestselling author of *Hands Free Mama, Only Love Today,* and *Live Love Now*

"This engaging book is a wonderful series of gentle, compassionate reminders of the role we play in our children's lives. Bridgett Miller shows us how much a touch of perspective can help in guiding our path as parents. She aptly fleshes out how seeing our children correctly leads us to becoming the parents our children need."

Gordon Neufeld, PhD developmental psychologist and founder of the Neufeld Institute

"A treasure for all who love and care for children. The affirmations and practical suggestions will enrich anyone who wants to better understand how to support children's emotional health and well-being. A gentle and compassionate parenting guide."

Mona Delahooke, PhD pediatric psychologist and author of *Beyond Behaviors: Using Brain Science and Compassion to Understand and Solve Children's Behavioral Challenges*

"I've trusted Bridgett Miller's advice for years. This refreshingly honest and empowering book is a beautiful culmination of her important work. I'm convinced that, with this book in hand, parents can confidently raise emotionally healthy, happy, and secure children."

Rebecca Eanes author of *Positive Parenting: An Essential Guide*

"Brimming with actionable steps, positive affirmations, and relatable anecdotes, Bridgett Miller's *What Young Children Need You to Know* is a concise and practical guide to getting to know your children's inner world."

L.R. Knost author of *Two Thousand Kisses a Day: Gentle Parenting Through the Ages and Stages*

"A well-written, thought-provoking, and inspiring book of affirmations backed up by science, research, and Bridgett Miller's personal experience. Highly recommended."

Jessica Joelle Alexander bestselling author of *The Danish Way of Parenting: What the Happiest People in the World Know About Raising Confident, Capable Kids*

"An actionable guide to letting go of our fears and seeing children through a new lens, which allows us to get curious about behaviour instead of feeling overwhelmed by it."

Lori Petro author and founder of TEACH Through Love

"A realistic, heart-centred understanding of children and their physical and emotional needs. This book reminds us to trust the goodness of children, to trust ourselves as parents, and to trust the human heart."

Pennie Brownlee child and parent advocate, education consultant, and author

"Bridgett Miller's tone will soothe beleaguered moms and dads while reassuring them that they (and their children) are doing just fine. If there's any doubt, the brilliant know-how inside will guide the way."

Sarah MacLaughlin, LSW author of *What Not to Say: Tools for Talking with Young Children*

"Bridgett Miller's book dances the reader right into the hearts and minds of children. I will be recommending this book to all of my clients!"

Dr. Vanessa Lapointe R.Psych, author

"A beautifully written, engaging, and encouraging book for parents."

Genevieve Simperingham dip. psychosynthesis counselling, certified parent educator, and instructor and co-founder of the Peaceful Parent Institute

"Keep this book on hand for those times when you either need a perspective shift and/or have a rare spare few minutes! Read a short chapter as bedtime reading, and let Bridgett Miller change how you see your child, so you can help them flourish."

Jacqueline Green founder of the Great Parenting Simplified movement

"This essential guide should be in the hands of every busy parent who is on the path of conscious parenting. *What Young Children Need You to Know* is down to earth, heart-centred, rooted in developmental science, and most importantly, deeply compassionate."

Anna Seewald, M.Ed keynote speaker, author, parent educator, and host of the *Authentic Parenting* podcast

"This book is practical, deeply insightful, and based on relational developmental science. Bridgett Miller offers us an immense gift in these pages, into the wonder of our children and the growth and gifts we receive by being their parents."

Julie Cusmariu certified life coach, intuitive consultant, and host and producer of *Julie in Conversation*

"This nurturing, educational book inspires deep reflection, compassion, and understanding, empowering the most vulnerable."

Lelia Schott gentle parenting advocate and founder of Synergy: gentle parenting resources

"Bridgett Miller does an incredible job of offering parents the opportunity to see things through a child's eyes, moment to moment, while at the same time showing the parent where compassion is needed, both for the self and the child."

Sue DeCaro worldwide life and parent coach

"This book is amazing! It would make such a difference in parents' lives if they would read even one chapter a day and practice its wisdom."

Vivek Patel conscious parenting educator and founder of Meaningful Ideas

"An engaging book that offers parents a refreshing and positive perspective on what can often be big challenges. This book holds just the right amount of valuable information and inspiration in each chapter, to avoid overloading busy parents."

Kirsty Lee child and parent advocate, and founder of Gentle Parenting Memes

"Just as a plane will arrive at a different destination if the pilot alters the flight trajectory by even one degree, parents who read Bridgett Miller's wise and bite-size observations about children's true nature and change how they respond to even one of their children's behaviours will find themselves in a more co-operative and connected place with their child."

Pam Leo author of *Connection Parenting*

"In *What Young Children Need You to Know*, Bridgett Miller's beautiful storytelling illustrates the everyday influence we have on our children. She reminds us that while we do not have control over who our children become, the relationship we build with them influences their sense of security and confidence, as well as their ability to think critically, responsibly, and compassionately about themselves, others, and the world around them. As I read Bridgett's book, I felt she understood the myriad of emotions, fears, and imperfections I experience as a mother. And while she acknowledges these hardships, she also gently holds me accountable to my role as the adult ... to soften my responses to my child and to myself, because from that softening comes strength and power. Bridgett acknowledges that parenting is *hard*, that we're going to be imperfect, and that when we better understand our children we are able to move forward from a place of love and understanding."

Amy C. Bryant, EdS, LPC psychotherapist at Wild Child Counseling and Parenting Beyond Punishment

"The minute I started reading this book I felt a blanket of love wrap around me and instantly comfort me with inspiration, courage, insight, and a wisdom that soothed my soul. I could see myself in *every* chapter and found deep, profound love for myself once again. I laughed. I cried... a lot. I remembered the value of the journey through parenthood, because I often forget. This book is a reminder to stay present, listen with your heart, and look for the love that is there—always. Bridgett Miller is a force of love on this planet and her book is pure genius."

Heather Criswell speaker, author, and entrepreneur

"In this touching book, Bridgett Miller led me on a magical journey to see through the innocent eyes of my child. She offers inspiration and guidance to trust the one gift I always longed to share... my wisdom. Through Bridgett's endless kindness, she illuminates the path alongside our children to experience the depth and profound effects of being seen, heard, and understood for who they are."

Leslie Potter parent coach at Purejoy Parenting

what young
children need ~~want~~
you to know

what young
children ~~want~~ need
you to know

how to see them so you know
what to do for them

bridgett miller

foreword by **DEBORAH MACNAMARA, PhD**

Look with
Love Press

ISBN 978-1-7770649-0-7 (paperback)
ISBN 978-1-7770649-1-4 (ebook)

Published by Look with Love Press
www.bridgettmiller.com

Produced by Page Two
www.pagetwo.com

Cover design by Prateeba Perumal
Cover photos by Taysia Louie and iStock
Interior design by Setareh Ashrafologhalai

www.bridgettmiller.com

To my daughters, Caite and Erin
Thank you for choosing me.

To my nephew, Little Ryan
Thank you for reminding
us that every day is precious.

xoxo

Contents

Foreword

I THINK MOTHER NATURE has a sense of humour—
at least you have to believe this when you consider
how different young children are from the adults
who raise them. While parents pride themselves in
feeling like a grown-up, they are routinely humbled and
returned to square one as they take responsibility for
raising a child. How does a person of such small stature,
limited vocabulary, and little worldly knowledge make *us*
think we don't know what we are doing?

The difference between adults and young children
is stark. Young children are unpredictable, don't think
twice, or consider all the options as adults must do. They
are emotionally driven and react instinctively, whereas
parents need to use logic and reason to navigate their
day-to-day life. Young children live in the moment and
are short-sighted, but parents have to consider the big
picture and long-term implications (like what happens
if you don't eat anything green). Young kids love to play,
which is endearing, but parents typically have more work
to do than time to get it done in. Young kids follow their

desires while adults focus on what is needed—like clean teeth, sleep, and consuming some fruits and vegetables. The bottom line is that young children are not like us and we can't remember being like them. From opposite ends of the maturity spectrum we come together for what feels like the longest and the shortest journey of our life. The irony is truly astounding. You may laugh or you may cry (I confess to having done both), but I am pretty sure that Mother Nature is having a chuckle at our expense.

The good news is Bridgett Miller is someone who knows a lot about the chasm that lies between a young child and their parent. Not only does she have depth and breadth when it comes to developmental science and what kids need to realize their human potential, she also has "worked in the trenches" as a preschool teacher. This marriage of both science and practice has made for a formidable combination. Bridgett is able to translate everyday issues with a young child into developmental science so that parents feel they are in the driver's seat in caring for their kids. This is no small feat. Many parenting experts are happy to tell parents what to do, but Bridgett wants more than this for you and your child. She wants you to understand why kids act the way they do so that you will know what they need from you. It is this passion that has infused each page in this book in her characteristically humble and gentle way. Bridgett's belief in parents as the answer for a child's most essential needs is one of the reasons I cherish her.

It was Bridgett's role as a parent educator and consultant that led our paths to first cross as colleagues at the Neufeld Institute, the non-profit organization led by Dr. Gordon Neufeld. It was here we joined forces and deepened our knowledge from one of the world's leading attachment and developmental theorists, Gordon Neufeld. We share a belief that when adults understand the importance of right relationships and soft hearts they will be moved to provide what their children truly need. We believe in parents and we believe that young children are some of the most amazing people around. In short, we love kids and care deeply about helping their parents raise them.

So, what is our role as parents in raising our children and how will this book help you? I am convinced that if we see ourselves as playing midwife to the developmental potential that resides in each of our children, we will be less tormented in thinking that everything is our responsibility to teach, correct, or get on top of. If we understand that nature provides a blueprint for our children to grow when the conditions are right, then we will focus more on fostering these conditions rather than hurrying our kids to talk right, act right, and simply "just grow up." If we understand that our children are born with the capacity to become resilient, resourceful, overcome challenges, think for themselves, have goals and passions, care about others, develop impulse control, manage their emotions, and form meaningful relationships, we will ask the question: "how do I help this along?" instead of pushing them to get along. We will hear their statements of "I do it myself" as the birthplace of personhood instead of a test of our authority or of our competence as a parent.

If we really understand nature's intentions for growing our children up, we will be more at ease in our parenting role, happier to slow down and enjoy the moments, and realize that everything they need is already inside of us to give. We will feel more confident that nature trusts us to get this right even though we don't always have all the answers.

What we can easily lose sight of while absorbed in the tasks that come with caring for a young child, is that our days are numbered when it comes to being their primary caretaker. Our children never need us the same way like when they are little. My own children are teenagers now and I have felt myself moving toward a consulting role and placing the steering wheel for their life in their hands. I am now the one filled with separation anxiety as I think about a house without small feet running to find me, no bedtime chats about the things that only small people find interesting, and the silence that is coming to take over the places my kids played and giggled. What I no longer seem to remember are the hard nights when I was so tired I couldn't read another story (there were many), or the dirty dishes that called me while my children erupted in tantrums over the smallest things.

The biggest gift you will receive from Bridgett's book, if you really let it sink in, is to slow down enough to consider the beauty of the young child and the wonder that comes with being the one to raise them. As you return to this book in small doses or big ones, Bridgett's voice will be here to help you cherish your young child despite whatever frustration you or they may be feeling. It is her insight into a young child that is the truest gift on these pages.

Like riding a bike, being a parent is something you have to learn by sitting in the saddle. Someone can give you all the advice you need and more, but there is something about having to do it for yourself that makes the learning come to life. As a parent you may find yourself veering one direction in being firm with your expectations, rules, and noes. Perhaps you are the type of parent who is more likely to veer in another direction where your children experience only compassion and warmth in spite of their immature ways. The challenge is to find the place in the middle where you can be both caring and firm. It is here you will be able to set boundaries while making room for their emotions and preserving your relationship. You will be able to lead your child without exploiting their dependency on you through contrived discipline like time outs, 1-2-3 magic, or consequences (which are pointless with young kids who don't think twice in the first place). When you can parent a child from a place of caring and feeling responsible for making the necessary decisions on their behalf, then your children will surely follow you. As Gordon Neufeld often states, your children never feel lost when they are sure of the person who is leading them.

Bridgett's book is like a GPS that is here to accompany you on the parenting ride. As your guide, I can assure you she has travelled this path before. She isn't afraid of young children, from the messes they create, to the loud emotions they have, or the frustration you may feel. She knows that there is nothing like the force of a young child, in all their glorious ways of being, that will bring out all the immature ways still left inside of you. As a parent to two young adults herself, Bridgett knows that nature will take care of growing our children up if we do our job to help her. She also knows that nature helps us grow to be the parent our children need—a gift that comes back to us as we strive to make sense of our kids and be the one they call "home."

You and your young children are in such wonderful hands with my dear friend Bridgett Miller.

Deborah MacNamara, PhD
January 2020

Introduction

I F YOU'VE BEEN drawn to pick up this book, it may be because you have young children and you're tired, possibly frustrated, and maybe even doubting yourself. Perhaps you're worried about their behaviour or feeling unsure of how to support them, and you're wondering if they'll ever grow out of it. Or it might just be that you're curious about what makes young children do the things they do and you want to understand them better. If any of these motivations led you here, this book has been written for you.

This book doesn't offer you step-by-step solutions, and it's not a manual on how to change your children's behaviour. Rather, it offers insight on connecting your head to your heart and supporting you on your conscious parenting journey. Sometimes, just shifting our perspective and attempting to understand what young children's behaviour is trying to tell us, is what's needed to inspire us to change *our* ways so that we can nurture our shared connection as we support their growing up.

Young children are driven by emotion. They're exuberantly joyful, enormously lovable, incredibly unpredictable, often inconsiderate, frequently resistant, and many other things in between. They live in the moment and their behaviour is trying to let us know how they're feeling. Our responsibility is to learn how to read their behaviour because they're still developing the communication skills to tell us what they want and need. That's where this book comes in.

Observing and trying to understand children's behaviour has been a passion of mine for a very long time. I've been a preschool and kindergarten teacher, remedial therapist, parent educator, and, most important, a parent for almost two decades. During this time, I've been approached by countless parents who've asked me questions about what to do with their children in order to get them to change their behaviour.

This book is my response to many of those questions. But rather than prescribing what to *do*, I've shifted the focus onto how to *see* children, because once we understand what's moving them to behave in the ways they are, we naturally start to meet their needs rather than wasting energy on trying to manipulate their behaviour.

Studying to become a teacher introduced me to the expansive world of child development and learning theory. It afforded me the opportunity to test theory out in the classroom and on the playground. This hands-on experience has been pivotal in allowing me to see that although theory can be helpful, we must never lose sight of the fact that children are unique and must be respected as the individuals they are.

My search to make sense of my own young children's behaviour led me to discover the work of the internationally acclaimed developmental psychologist Gordon

Neufeld. His endeavours are based on the understanding that the context for raising children is their attachment to those responsible for them. This attachment-based, developmental approach to making sense of children's behaviour helped me connect the dots between what I had learned and observed over the years and how to integrate it with what my heart always knew to be true. I am filled with gratitude every day for being in the right place at the right time, and for being gifted the incredible opportunity to be invited into the presence of such a brilliant, kind-hearted gentleman who has dedicated his life to supporting adults in making sense of the children in their lives.

As a teacher and as a parent, I have come to see that every interaction is an invitation to teach and to learn. As adults, we may think we're primarily here to teach, but I now know the children in my life show up exactly when I need a reminder that I still have much learning and growing up to do. Although adults may have the edge on young children regarding life experience and knowledge, children run circles around many of us when it comes to living in the present moment, feeling whatever it is they feel, and expressing themselves authentically. While we often admire these qualities, we may at times dislike them because they stir up emotions that we may otherwise have been able to avoid if young children weren't sent as the messengers.

Over the years, parents have shared with me that coming to understand their children's behaviour a little better has shifted their perception regarding what moves them, and their children, to behave in the ways they do. Seeing young children as creatures of emotion and attachment in need of our help to navigate their big feelings, as opposed to assuming they are being obstinate and purposefully difficult, empowers parents to transform their reactions into responses. Not every time, but more of the time. Realizing that young children need adults to help them to move through their big emotions—rather than having their behaviour clamped down upon—has unexpectedly led many parents to start paying attention to what's going on inside of themselves when they're feeling stirred up and are tempted to act out in immature ways.

As adults, we have a choice to make regarding how we treat children. An awareness of this freedom to choose can inspire us to look at our behaviour and then, if need be, to seek insight and support to help bring our behaviour into alignment with our heartfelt intentions. When doing so, a surge in self-awareness can lead parents to discover new depths of patience and an increased capacity to show more compassion. For some, having an innocent child look to them for love and rely on them for guidance opens them up to seeing what their child needs and what may be lacking inside of themselves. This startling revelation can be immensely upsetting, but may become the impetus behind finding the strength and courage needed to be there for children in ways they wish someone would have done for them when they were growing up.

Parenting can become a daily reminder of the importance of getting to know ourselves better so that we can become more conscious in all of our relationships. I've written this book with the intention of building a bridge between developmental science and conscious parenting, which is a collection of beliefs about what children need to develop and thrive, not a prescriptive set of rules for parents to follow. Although some people joke that any parent who is not asleep is conscious, perhaps, while reading this book, they'll sense that something profound is going on, and parenting may just be the invitation they've been waiting for in order to awaken their deeper sense of self.

Many parents are experiencing a sense of "coming home" when introduced to the idea of conscious parenting. They intuitively know that young children thrive in the context of connection and learn best through gentle guidance and correction. Emphasis is placed on recognizing and meeting the child's emotions as they are in the moment, rather than trying to coercively control them. Parents are encouraged to pay attention to how they are feeling and to come alongside their child by acknowledging their child's upset and frustration, without being sucked in and overwhelmed by their own. It's in this space that parents discover they don't need to parent punitively because children learn and flourish when treated with respect, understanding, and compassion.

The conscious parenting movement, primarily driven by the impassioned endeavours of Dr. Shefali Tsabary, is steadily gathering momentum and more parents are recognizing that their relationship with their children is so much more than what was once viewed by many as a traditional obligation and responsibility to merely get their children to behave in socially appropriate ways. When we embrace parenting as a conscious partnership between parent and child, we find ourselves on a journey that benefits us all in serendipitous ways.

The common thread running through each page in this book is the importance of putting the heart connection and relationship we have with children ahead of wanting to take practical action to teach them. Once we understand and appreciate just how much children need a deep sense of connection and sense of being loved, we're better positioned to trust ourselves to interact in ways that preserve and grow our relationship ahead of trying to change children's immature behaviour. To do so, parents often have to release the deluded notion that children are here to make us happy and that their behaviour needs to be a certain way in order for us to experience the joy of parenting. For me, releasing this misperception has been one of the most difficult but freeing experiences of my life, and my children's inherently immature behaviour no longer feels like a yardstick to measure my happiness and sense of self-worth.

Consciously recognizing that our children are not responsible for our happiness can empower us to start seeing them as being here to help us to face the uninvited parts of ourselves that we haven't yet explored or integrated. While their pleasant behaviours bring out the best in us, too much of this can lull us into the false belief that we don't still have growing up to do. All interactions, especially the most challenging ones are, I believe, perfect opportunities to foster continued growth and expansion in adults.

Finding and keeping the joy in parenting requires parents to figure out the balance between being there for their children and doing things for themselves. Many worn-out parents believe that what they are lacking is more "me time," only to discover that no amount of time away can alleviate the tension that comes with being a parent. The childish behaviours we're wanting to have a break from will still exist when we return. That's why putting some of our energy into understanding the needs that drive young children's behaviours and then doing what we can to meet them, will—in the long term—serve us much better than a weekend away at a spa.

Parents certainly need time for themselves and have to get resourceful about doing so, especially when they don't have a circle of support readily accessible. In generations gone by, parents typically had family members to support and assist them with raising their children but nowadays that's more the exception than the norm. As such, we also need to find ways to nurture ourselves and restore our energy in the presence of our young children if we are to avoid resenting them for having to rely on us to meet their every need.

Becoming more mindful of our ways can bring a sense of calm to the chaos that often accompanies taking care of young children. When we start paying attention to the chatter in our heads, we may notice it's the quality of the repetitive self-talk that drags us down because our thoughts become our beliefs. Constantly telling ourselves that parenting is such hard work, that we're so tired, and that we don't know how much more of this we can take, saps our energy and leaves us feeling depleted and despondent.

It's easy to be distracted by young children's behaviours, especially those that fall outside of our hopes and expectations. Parents are usually quick to notice the shortcomings of young children and less likely to acknowledge how much they have matured and learned in a relatively short time. Where our attention goes, our energy flows. By focusing more on their progress rather than on how far they still have to go, we're more likely to align our parenting ways with meeting their needs and nurturing their pure potential.

Whenever we intentionally notice the little things that young children do to delight us, they pull us into their world where even the most ordinary things seem marvellous. When we slow down and join them in the here and now rather than blindly rushing through the day, checking off things on our to-do lists, we can't help but find more pleasure and appreciation in what they have to offer. This book reminds us to notice young children's innocence and their innate ability to live in the moment, and encourages us to sometimes do the same.

For as long as I can remember, an essential part of my well-being has included taking time for my spiritual practice and making the time to exercise. As a tired and busy mother of young children, there were stretches when this fell by the wayside, but I noticed that not making the time left me feeling somewhat untethered. For many parents, establishing a daily practice of movement, gratitude, and taking a few attentive seconds to notice all the goodness that surrounds us not only inspires us to show up more fully and kindly for ourselves and others, it allows us to do so with more compassion and grace.

Each entry in this book has been written with the intention of perhaps changing the way you look at children's behaviour, because when you do, what you see will change. It will still be the same child in front of you, behaving in the same immature ways, but you'll have a different perception of why they're acting out in the ways they are, and you'll respond to their needs with more understanding, patience, and kindness. In time, many of the struggles you've been having will begin to right themselves—not because of any technique you've used, but because of how you now see, connect, and relate to your unique child.

Whenever you pick up this book, I hope you'll feel as though you're having a conversation with a caring friend who can relate to some of the joys, struggles, and worries you're encountering on your parenting journey. Although no two paths are identical, sometimes just hearing another's story and perspective is all that's needed to inspire us to keep showing up instead of giving up.

On behalf of your young children, thank you for all you do for them and for taking the time to refer to this book as often as you feel drawn to it. As with all I share, please only take what makes sense to your head or resonates with your heart, or both. Leave the rest behind.

With love,
Bridgett

How to Use
This Book

. . . .

THIS BOOK IS about looking at children with love, because love is all there is, and children are here to remind us of that. Each entry is a quick and easy read for parents who only have a few minutes and want a hit of inspiration and insight to keep them on their path of becoming the parent and person they long to be.

There is no specific sequence in which to read the entries. You may choose to read them in page order, one per day, or however you like. Perhaps on some days you'll choose to pick it up and open it to a random page . . . then that's the page meant for you!

Each entry opens with a statement that a young child might make. I refer to this as the "inspiration." Pay attention to the feeling you experience when you read it. If the inspiration statement resonates with you and draws you in, you're meant to read on. If not, turn to a different page and see how you feel about that inspiration statement. If none resonate with you, this book is not meant for you today. Never feel obligated to read on; tomorrow is another day.

If the inspiration statement speaks to you, read the body of the entry, which I refer to as the "insight." This section offers hints of developmental and attachment theory on the topic. I've included some personal parenting stories and some tales from my experiences as a teacher to help illustrate and clarify the insight. Don't focus too much on trying to understand what you read; if it feels right as you're reading it, the understanding will naturally follow.

Each entry includes a "Here's what you can do..." paragraph that can help you set your intention for future interactions. It's not meant as a prescription to follow, but to promote an awareness of what children need so you can be more present with them in the future. Once you begin to see children as needing your love and gentle guidance, you'll naturally feel empowered to respond with more kindness and compassion and the relationship you share will deepen. This can't be learned, and it can't be forced; it must be felt.

Finally, the entry concludes with a parenting affirmation. This one-liner distills the entry to its essence and gives you a tangible intention to help guide you on your parenting journey. It's not meant to try and get you to think positively; instead, it's a sentence you can return to when you're needing a reminder about where to focus your attention. Little, consistent, conscious steps forward will take you where you want to go. Your heart already knows where that is.

For daily inspiration, updates, and events, please visit me at www.bridgettmiller.com or follow me on social media:

Facebook @look.with.love.bridgett and @parenting.with.intention.bridgett or on Instagram @lookwithlove_bridgett and @parentingwithintention. If you love what you see, please share it with those you care about.

Serenity Invocation for Parents

Grant me *the eyes* to see
what is driving my child to behave
in the ways they are;

A *soft heart* to show them my
kindness when they need it most;

And sufficient *patience* for me to
guide us through each moment,

So we both *emerge* better for it.

1. Who I Grow Up to Become Isn't Completely Up to You

WHEN MY first daughter was just a few days old, I remember waking up in the middle of the night with what felt like a huge weight pressing down on my chest. As I sat up in bed, gasping for air, it hit me: I was now fully responsible for another human being's well-being. Up until this moment I'd been preparing myself in theory, but now that my daughter had arrived, the reality of this enormous responsibility was overwhelming.

None of us can fully comprehend what will be required of us as parents until we become one.

We may have an inkling of what to expect based on the stories we've been told and from the child-parent inter-actions we've personally experienced, but the sense of accountability that accompanies our bundle of joy cannot be accurately predicted. Nothing can adequately prepare us for how exciting and overwhelming it is to become a parent. I remember those first weeks being filled with mixed feelings as I celebrated my daughter's presence while wondering if I was up for the job.

As children grow and develop, our responsibilities shift and expand. At first, we need to keep them safe, warm, fed, and filled up with love. As they get older, we also begin to prepare them to take their place in the social world. We need to teach them right from wrong, impart our morals and values, and, to some extent, teach them about society's behavioural expectations. Over time, our ever-increasing parental responsibilities may begin to feel more like a heavy burden and less like a calling. We try and raise children who remain true to themselves while also fitting in with the cultural norms so they don't feel excluded because they're too different.

The mounting pressure to try and do it all not only keeps us busy, it also leads us away from being able to trust that raising children hasn't been left completely up to us. While we may not all have an extensive network of helping hands and supportive adults at the ready, we each have a powerful, invisible helper on our side. Our assistant is a force greater than we could ever imagine: Mother Nature.

In the busy-ness of the day-to-day duties of parenting, it's helpful to take a moment to consider the natural development taking place inside of every child. Although we innately trust that an acorn will someday grow into an oak tree without requiring any formal instruction, we are hesitant to trust that nature has a crucial role to play in the natural unfolding of our children.

Remember that your child's development hasn't been left completely up to you. You're certainly responsible for providing the nurturing conditions for healthy development to occur, but it is ultimately nature that will get the job done. Think of yourself as the willing assistant who manages the day-to-day affairs of your child, while nature silently works on the inside of each child, cultivating them into the mature adults they are on their way to becoming. When we begin to see our children as growing and evolving rather than needing to be trained and taught, we are on our way to prioritizing and nurturing their need for closeness and connection as these are the conditions in which everything else will take root and then flourish.

....

Here's what you can do...

Always remember that who your child grows up to become isn't completely dependent on you. By assuming that you're the one who has to teach them everything and that you need to get it all right, you put tremendous pressure on yourself and unnecessary stress on your child. Remind yourself nature has a plan, and you'll need to trust it if you are to experience more of the true joy that comes from loving and taking care of a child.

....

Today's parenting affirmation: I will keep in mind that nature has a perfect plan for my child.

2. I Didn't Come with a Manual— and That's a Good Thing

THE ANTICIPATION of becoming a parent seems to bring out the researcher in many of us. We can't resist the powerful allure of books and resources offering a glimpse of what might be waiting on the other side of welcoming a child to this world. To become well-informed, we're driven to sift through heaps of information in an attempt to learn as much as we can in preparation for parenthood. What many of us don't know is that what we're really searching for isn't to be found in resources; it's a sense of confidence that's waiting to be stirred within us as we get to know our children.

As a parent, you've likely also found yourself second-guessing your actions with your children. We wonder what exactly we're supposed to be doing to convey everything we think our offspring need to learn. If only each child arrived clutching a manual containing instructions on how to go about raising them to be happy, healthy, confident children who, thanks to our dedicated efforts, grow up to become mature, responsible, balanced adults.

If ever you've wished for such a manual, it's because you take your responsibility of raising a child seriously. You yearn to do right by the children you love. You may also carry a niggling doubt that you shouldn't rely solely on your inner guidance because we live in an age where so many esteemed experts can be accessed with a click of a button. More than that, it's possible you don't completely trust that you will indeed begin to figure out what is needed from you as your child grows and the relationship you share begins to unfold. It's this insecurity that sometimes leads us astray and tempts us to search for solutions outside of ourselves rather than look within for some answers.

While many of us start reading "what to expect"-type books in anticipation of becoming parents, our hunger for clear answers from outside experts doesn't really begin to gather momentum until we become hands-on parents and we repeatedly find ourselves in the middle of what feel like desperate and defining parenting moments. Of course, there is something to be said for wanting to get ahead by preparing for what's potentially coming down the line, but the reality is, we don't know what will be expected of us until we find ourselves right in the middle of it.

The upside of not having a manual—and it's a big one—is that it releases us from comparing our children with those who live in a textbook. This relieves us of worries about problems that may never materialize and empowers us to focus instead on seeing the child in front of us for who they truly are rather than tempting us to focus on who they are not.

Your determination to find answers is admirable, but accessing too much information can become a double-edged sword. Acquired knowledge may serve you well if what you learn unfolds according to what experts say is the norm, but it may feel like a stab in the heart when it doesn't. Accepting that there isn't a single book or resource that offers complete and accurate insight into your unique child may feel unsettling, but it's also the key to unlocking the door to begin trusting yourself to capably raise your children by relying on both your head and your heart.

....

Here's what you can do...

Trust that you have the ability to see your child for who they truly are. By getting to know them, you will begin to understand them and, in doing so, start to read them. Prescribed instructions on how to interact with children may sound appealing, but they limit your ability to respond to your child as the individual they are, and this affects the relationship you're cultivating. Development is a natural process and watching them closely and getting to know who they truly are will serve both of you better than any manual.

....

Today's parenting affirmation: I do not need a manual; I need to trust myself.

3. My Behaviour Isn't Always a Reflection of Your Parenting Skills

TRYING TO calm your child having a meltdown in the middle of a busy supermarket is the stuff parental nightmares are made of. It's the sort of thing you half-heartedly anticipate because you know it's what young children do, but there's a little part of you that secretly hopes you'll be the one who figures out how to raise a child who doesn't misbehave and publicly humiliate you.

The first time I endured a raucous toddler throw-down in public was in aisle number five at our local grocery store. Our outing had gone really well, and I had just a few more items to get before heading to the checkout. I'd managed to keep my daughter entertained in the cart as we wound our way through the store, but she reached a point where she no longer found my efforts captivating. She began to fuss and complain, and I explained that we wouldn't be there very much longer. I sped up and tried to distract her, but as the minutes ticked by her objections grew louder and she let out a piercing scream that seemed to run on a loop. Other shoppers began staring, so I held my ground and explained to her through gritted teeth that we were almost done. That didn't appease her one bit as she was already too far gone. She upped her volume and began thrashing around in the cart like a child possessed. It felt like a crowd of gawking spectators was gathering to watch the show. Their glares hit me like burning arrows and I imagined their mutterings were criticisms of my inability to control my unruly child.

It wasn't long before a lady in her late sixties began walking toward me and I froze. I was quite sure she was heading over to admonish me for my child's disruptive behaviour, and if not that, to offer me some unsolicited advice on how to deal with my child's disorderly conduct. I braced myself for the humiliation she was about to heap on top of my distress and embarrassment. She locked eyes with me and then she said, "My dear, what can I do to help you?" I almost burst into tears. I hadn't expected her kindness and understanding because I felt so unworthy of it. Despite my best efforts, I hadn't been able to calm my child's protest, and I was feeling excruciatingly incompetent. This lady could see it. Only then did it occur to me that I was being unreasonably hard on myself and on my child because I was expecting behaviour from her that was beyond her current developmental capacity to deliver.

That lovely lady's compassionate words were enough to bring me to my senses. Suddenly the severity of this perceived disaster seemed more manageable because I knew that I wasn't alone in this moment. A complete stranger had reached out to me and although she couldn't undo what was already done or make my child behave any better, she had softened my heart and opened my eyes. I could now see that my little girl wasn't being intentionally belligerent, she was letting me and everyone else know that she was done with being at the store for today. There was nothing shameful about that and I knew just what to do. I thanked the kind lady for her caring offer, assured her that we were fine, and I abandoned the loaded-up cart right there in aisle number five. My priorities had shifted; the groceries could wait. We went home and ate toast together for dinner.

More often than we may realize, the people around us are not judging us, they're onlookers who are really thankful they're not the ones in the predicament we're in. Parenting requires us to practise not allowing ourselves to be derailed by the stares and comments of others when our children are acting out. Knowing there will be times when even our best efforts cannot circumvent the inevitable makes it more likely that we'll find our way through the difficult, trying, and embarrassing situations without acting out in ways that do a disservice to the children we love and the relationship we're building with them.

Here's what you can do...

Just because you can't always direct your child doesn't mean that you're a parenting failure. It means you're still learning how to interact with them in their current developmental state, and they're still working toward developing self-control. Keep your focus on what's going on for them rather than being distracted by those around you. Any time you pay more attention to what others may (or may not) be thinking about you, you're being pulled away from seeing what your child needs and that's when you're more likely to do or say things that are out of alignment with your heartfelt intentions.

Today's parenting affirmation: My child is doing the best they can and so will I.

4. Don't Take Me Personally

MANY PARENTS are concerned by their young children's apparent lack of consideration for the feelings of others, especially when they hear their child hurl hurtful words at the people they profess to love the most. Being on the receiving end of a seething four-year-old who isn't getting their own way can be a rattling experience. I've had many moments like this, but the one that will stay with me forever was when I was first told by my daughter in no uncertain terms that she hated me and wished I was "deaded" so that she could have a new mommy! I was taken off guard by the intensity of her words. It didn't make sense to me that my typically loving and caring child could, at the flip of a switch, become so hostile and hurtful.

Without some developmental insight into where this behaviour is coming from, parents may be worried by the vehement words spewing from their child. Young children live in the moment because their developing brains are currently wired to experience only one pure emotion at a time. When they are happy, they are ecstatic, and when they are mad, they are downright fuming. Their behaviour is their communication.

Adults are typically troubled by young children's tendency to flip from one extreme to the other, particularly when that shift is accompanied by hurtful or socially inappropriate rhetoric. In these trying moments we may be distracted by their insensitive expressions of dissatisfaction, and we attempt to shut down their tirade of insults rather than see the developmental reasoning behind why they are so unapologetically brazen.

We need to remember that the immature brain is not yet sufficiently integrated* to allow young children to consider the impact of their words at the same time as they express how they are feeling. They are moved to speak before they think, just as they are moved to act ahead of considering the potential consequences of their actions. Adults who don't know this may incorrectly assume the child's malicious behaviour is premeditated and may therefore feel obligated to discipline harshly in order to stifle their outburst and get them to see the error in their disrespectful ways. We need to resist this knee-jerk reaction if we are to avoid causing a commotion and risk missing out on teaching them how to express their emotions in healthier and less offensive ways.

The starting place for dealing with any seemingly disrespectful talk is to remember that the child's words aren't personal; they are untamed expressions of immaturity. Young children's brains usually need five-to-seven years of good development for integration to take place, and in the case of more sensitive children, the brain may need between seven and nine years. While hurtful words can be wounding, it's our responsibility as mature adults to manage our reaction to what they say in the heat of the moment. We must keep in mind that when the child is frustrated, their words are an attempt to communicate

---

* For more information about the integration process and how young children mature, see page 203.

their frustration, and they can't yet help themselves. This is why we're called names like "poo-poo head" and our longevity is coldly cursed by them. If we start to feel personally attacked by their angry words, we may respond in ways that parallel those of the immature child.

If we do nothing but bite our tongues and remind ourselves that it's their immaturity speaking and it's not personal, we're on our way to being able to teach them what we want them to learn in ways that will benefit their long-term growth and development. We can't teach them in that very moment, but we can and must talk to them about more effective and appropriate ways to express themselves once their frustration has subsided.

Understanding that their brain is still under construction empowers us to take their behaviour less personally and to back off without sabotaging the relationship we are building with them. As they mature and their brain begins to integrate, they will start to mix their emotions and will express themselves in a more civilized fashion. Until then, our focus needs to be on loving them through it all and making sure we're modelling the behaviour we hope to someday see in them.

Here's what you can do...

While you most certainly need to teach your children how to behave in ways that will help them to one day fit into society, resist trying to put the cart before the horse. Attempting to teach a young child something they aren't yet capable of doing fuels a sense of disconnection between you and your child. When your child is frustrated and they call you hurtful names or disrespect you in some way, remember they're being moved by their big emotions and don't yet know how to control their expression. It's not personal; it's an indication of their developmental immaturity. With your understanding and loving guidance they will get there, but until they do, be sure to model the language and behaviour you'd one day like to see in them.

Today's parenting affirmation: My immature child is not deliberately trying to hurt my feelings.

5. I'm Going to Take You to Unexplored Parts of Yourself

I WAS a teacher for almost a decade before having my own two daughters, and although I had years of hands-on experience with young children, becoming a parent was an enormous adjustment. In some aspects, I was right about what to expect, but there was a monsoon of unforeseen emotion that welled up inside of me. I quickly realized that no matter who I was or how prepared I thought I was, being a parent is a humbling experience, and we all have to figure out how to do it on the job. While those who have come before us may try and prepare us for the road ahead with their tales, anecdotes, and warnings, their words can't fully sink in because we don't have any personal parenting experience to relate them to.

Regardless of how our children come to be part of our lives, once they're in our presence and we commit our hearts to being responsible for their long-term well-being, things start to get real quickly. What is expected, or sometimes demanded, from us is revealed in our day-to-day interactions as they begin to grow up. During the easygoing times, their rapid development evokes a sense of awe and wonder within us, but in the trying times, we're overcome with bouts of frustration, worry, guilt, and exhaustion.

As such, dedicated but worn-out parents often begin to question their ability to meet the needs of their children, particularly during interactions that challenge and test their physical and emotional limits. Being human means there are times when we're pushed to the brink of what we think we can handle, and it's here where so many parents recognize themselves as falling short of their heartfelt intentions. Whenever we act in ways that are outside of the behavioural ideals we hold, we can't help but doubt our ability to raise the children who manage to provoke us in ways few others ever have.

Young children have a way of leading us to explore the emotional territory inside of ourselves that we've previously never had the need or motivation to investigate. When we find ourselves feeling as though we're going to be tipped over the edge by their apparent unwillingness to do things the way we want and when we want, we're being invited to go deeper within ourselves to keep our actions in alignment with our heartfelt intentions. It's our caring heart and commitment to their well-being that move us to expand our tolerance and adjust our expectations in order to preserve and deepen the connection we have with them.

When we're willing to look at our shortcomings and see them as opportunities for further growth rather than as rigid limitations that define us, we're on the way to discovering unexplored depths of perseverance, patience, and personal expansion. We come to see that our children are not obstacles in our lives, they're the invitations we've been waiting for to inspire us to really start living our best lives.

Here's what you can do...

When you're faced with a child whose behaviour is stirring you up in ways that push you to the brink of what you think you can tolerate, take a few seconds to remind yourself that this infuriating interaction is an opportunity to notice immature parts of yourself; even more important, it's an invitation to see what your child needs from you in this very moment. By putting your focus on what it is you can do for them, and finding ways to meet their needs, you'll spontaneously grow yourself up as you support them to do the same.

Today's parenting affirmation: I am open to growing up further, alongside my child.

6. I Need You to Understand Me

....

CONVERSATIONS WITH young children are often unpredictable experiences. We never quite know what they are going to say next and sometimes they have us in stitches of laughter because of the words or pronunciation they use. Other times, it may be very difficult to make sense of what they're trying to communicate and as their frustration rises, so does ours. Every parent has likely had occasions where they're desperately trying to extract meaning from their child, with limited success. In these moments we should become mindful of how we're handling the situation because sometimes we're inadvertently escalating it and making it more challenging than it needs to be.

When young children get excited or overwhelmed it's typical for them to speed up their speech, get louder, or become more animated. This can make it tricky to decode what they are saying. It can be tempting to try and control their harried speech by making well-meaning suggestions like "Use your words" or "Calm down," but this frustrates them even more and their urgency escalates. As they get more agitated, the more discombobulated their speech becomes. Their verbal frustration may begin to morph into acts of physical expression to which we respond impatiently.

Keep in mind that not every interaction needs to be used as an opportunity to teach children something. When they're excited or upset and are stumbling over their words, we need to listen intently rather than correcting their grammar or articulation. We also need to listen beneath their words in an attempt to connect with the emotion that is driving them to speak or act out. Whatever they are trying to communicate is important to them, and what they need most from us is to know they are being heard and we will do our best to understand. Of course, there are times when we honestly don't know what they're saying, but even then, we should be aware of never making them feel as though what they're expressing is insignificant.

Children who aren't feeling heard or understood experience a deep sense of disconnection, and this may result in them acting out aggressively toward those around them or turning it inwardly on themselves. Lashing out at others or hurting themselves is an indication that the child's level of frustration has surpassed their ability to contain it. To an onlooker, the child may seem rude and unruly when really, all they are is frustrated about not feeling understood.

In these instances, using too many words is not necessary, nor is it helpful. As best we can, we should dial down our ways in attempt to stay connected and help them settle. Most young children respond well to some light physical contact as this helps to ground them when they're upset. Sometimes just reaching out your hand and touching them lightly, or extending your arm and gently drawing them toward you, can add some calm to the equation. Other times, giving them a little space makes all the difference.

That said, it's always our responsibility to read the child and the situation carefully and predict as best we can how our advances will be received. We must trust that we each know our own children best and although we attend to what they are saying, we must also pay close attention to what they are communicating without words as this will help us to respond to them in ways that allow them to feel more seen, heard, and understood.

Here's what you can do...

When your child is excited or upset, they can't help but stumble over their words and mix up their grammar. They don't need you to correct them; what they want most is for you to give them the sense that you "get" them, even when they are struggling to express themselves. There will be plenty of calm interactions in the future to teach them new vocabulary and correct their grammar, but for now, do what you can to give them the sense that they and what they say, really matters to you.

Today's parenting affirmation: I will listen and respond to my child with presence.

7. That Popular Parenting Technique May Not Work on Me

THE DESPERATE need for adult conversation was a great motivator to get my young children ready, dressed, and out the door. Taking them to the park was a win-win. For them it meant getting out into the fresh air, having space to run and play; for me it opened up the possibility of meeting other adults keen to chat using full sentences. There's something about the presence of children that naturally draws adults into conversation. Before long I was in the loop about other children's sleeping, eating, and pooping routines and was readily discussing and sharing opinions on topics I'd never imagined I'd be comfortable having with anyone—least of all strangers in the park! Parenting turns many of us into information-sharing enthusiasts, and almost every conversation revolves around how to raise children.

As parents, we tend to be on the lookout for tips on how to successfully help our children reach their full potential. The motivation for this is rooted in our desire to be a conscientious parent who provides the best conditions for children to thrive. These are honourable and purposeful intentions, but listening to too much well-meaning advice from other parents may be confusing and misleading.

On days when you feel your children are keeping pace with what appears to be the norm, you might casually chat with another parent, flip through a parenting magazine, or perhaps scroll through social media focused on development information. You do so out of interest and curiosity and aren't too invested in implementing the insight shared. You can take it or leave it.

In contrast, when you're feeling unsure of yourself or concerned that your child's development doesn't appear to be measuring up to their siblings or peers, you're driven to seek techniques to improve things. You're more susceptible to listening to advice and more likely to be tempted to try it out on your own child, especially if it comes with a hint of a promise that it might be the magic solution. Herein lies our introduction to the hamster wheel of conflicting and often misguiding information. Once we're on it, it can be extremely difficult to exit.

Whenever we take what-to-do directions from strangers, friends, family, or even experts, we usually lack the context in which the technique was originally implemented. Not knowing the context, we're unable to see the bigger picture and risk losing sight of the unique child. Just because a parenting method works on one child doesn't mean that it will work on yours. The procedure may seem clear, but the context is different and, as such, our heartfelt good intentions backfire far more frequently than they succeed.

I personally discovered this the hard way when following the specific steps recommended when implementing "time out" on my young daughter. The what-to-do was clear, but the reaction it evoked in her was certainly not the anticipated compliance so many others had attested to. If anything, it was the opposite. She resisted even more willfully and became completely unhinged and inconsolable. Regrettably, if the technique isn't working on the child, parents may either assume they are not implementing the technique correctly, or worse still, that there is something wrong with the child. Neither is accurate.

What was amiss was my unrelenting persistence. It blinded me from seeing that the technique I was using was preventing her from learning from me. I was withholding what she needed most from me in her upset state: a calm presence that held the boundary in place while also allowing her to feel her frustration and upset as she bumped up against it. As creatures of emotion, our greatest learning takes place when we're able to feel the sadness in what isn't working for us. Techniques that prevent children access to their vulnerability and sadness don't serve the child in the way we hope they will. Regardless of how well-intended, these techniques also steer parents away from listening to their hearts and as such, we risk implementing practices that work against our intuition and leave us and our children feeling disconnected and even more distraught.

Any time we resort to using seemingly quick-fix techniques, we inadvertently whittle away at the very core of what we need most to be able to effectively guide and teach our children: *our connection with them.* In the midst of our efforts to train children using contrived methods, we work against the deep relationship we want to cultivate with them. We don't intend to, but we make things much harder for ourselves and for our children.

Here's what you can do...

If parenting advice sounds too good to be true, it probably is. Pay close attention to how you feel in the seconds after you first hear about a new parenting method. Initially you may be intrigued, but if there is also a niggling sense of uneasiness inside of you, notice it before allowing yourself to be sucked in and convinced by the cold logic of a technique. Just because a method is popular and reportedly works on someone else's child, doesn't mean it's right for your child. Don't ignore your inner guidance and be tempted to implement strategies and techniques touted as quick fixes at the expense of the connection you want to have with your child.

Today's parenting affirmation: I will pay closer attention to what my intuition is telling me.

8. I Say What I Think

I'VE HAD my fair share of publicly embarrassing parenting moments. There have been occasions where my daughters have said or done something awkward, and we've managed to dismiss it as being innocently funny and move on. Other times have been less amusing, and I've wished the ground would open up and swallow us whole because not everyone understands or appreciates the candid ways of the immature.

Family and close friends don't usually take a child's blunt words too personally because they know and love the child. I remember my daughter asking her grandfather out of the blue why his nose was so big. He took it in stride and kindly replied that it helped him to smell things better. His quick-witted response became an inside joke between them, and they still laugh about it many years later. But not everyone has the same understanding.

I was once in a shopping mall when I heard a young child at the top of their voice inquire why a man was confined to a wheelchair. The boy's mother tried to quiet him down and quickly reached for his hand to subdue his pointing, but this only made the little guy more insistent that she answer his question. For some, this child's behaviour would be considered rude and offensive, but he was merely curious and had no concept of the potential impact his words might have on the feelings of others.

Unless we know that the young child's brain is not yet wired to be able to consider the impact of their words before blurting them out, we may assume they're being intentionally impolite or disrespectful. We may react harshly in an effort to curb their behaviour particularly if we're afraid of being judged for our child's seemingly rude or inconsiderate words. It may be our own embarrassment that moves us to admonish them or sternly demand they apologize, thereby escalating the situation way beyond what it ought to be.

In these awkward situations, all that is needed is for us to take the lead before childish actions are misunderstood and unwarranted words are exchanged. One way of doing so is to generously give an apology on our child's behalf and then move them along before any further upset occurs. Alternatively, if the person on the receiving end understands the context of what's just unfolded, they may choose to engage in a short conversation to explain a little more to our child about what piqued their curiosity. Depending on the situation, we might simply acknowledge the humour in the assumptions of the immature and share a knowing smile with the person before making a dash for the nearest exit.

It's after the incident that we'll have the opportunity to explain to our young child that sometimes what they say may come across as rude or hurtful to others. We can also convey our certainty that their actions weren't purposefully unkind and that we trust that as they grow older, they'll be more capable of keeping certain thoughts and words on the inside of their heads. By doing so, we protect their dignity and preserve our connection by not unfairly belittling them for their innocent mistakes. By using gentle words and actions we keep them open to learning from us, and we're better able to support them as they begin to navigate this complex social world.

. . . .

Here's what you can do...

Knowing that young children don't yet have the capacity to think before they speak empowers you to soften your response and to take responsibility for their immature actions. You'll feel more confident about taking the lead and circumventing any additional upset that may be provoked in others who do not understand what's going on developmentally for your child. When awkward situations arise—and they will—do what you can to normalize what's happened without shaming your child for their immature behaviour.

. . . .

Today's parenting affirmation: I will remember that immaturity makes my child seem inconsiderate.

9. You Might Not Like Me Some of the Time

. . . .

BEFORE BECOMING a parent, I found it difficult to grasp that anyone who loved their child could ever feel anything even close to dislike toward them. Looking back now, I can see that I unfairly judged parents who were honest enough to voice that sometimes they weren't feeling too fond of their own children. Back then it seemed to me they weren't being patient enough or they were being too quick to blame their children for their personal discontent. When I had two children of my own, I could then relate to why some tired, frustrated, or desperate parents sometimes have mixed feelings about their children.

The first time I recall being hit with a pang of aversion toward my own child was when we were stuck in a typical parent-child battle. I had repeatedly asked my young daughter to put on her shoes, and she had refused each time. The more forcefully I insisted, the more obstinate she became. She held her ground, broke off all eye contact, and then put her fingers in her ears to block me out. Her brazen audacity riled me and I remember thinking to myself, "I really don't like you very much right now." I was disappointed that I was capable of feeling this way toward a child I loved with all my heart and I felt riddled with guilt.

After a heart-to-heart conversation with a few good friends, I realized that I was not alone in experiencing these conflicted feelings. Up until that day, none of us had talked about this particular struggle. Openly sharing our experiences helped to normalize what was going on. We recognized that we still had the same range of emotions we'd had before becoming parents and, if anything, the presence of our children exacerbated the intensity of our emotions. Although we readily welcomed the intoxicating feelings of pure love our children stirred up in us, we agreed we were generally less accepting of the intense frustration they were able to provoke inside of us. Although we loved our children dearly, their childish behaviour sometimes had a way of stoking our frustration like few others ever had.

After that conversation, I could see I had a choice to make. I could either get stuck in a cycle of thinking it was my children I disliked whenever I felt triggered, or I could be courageous enough to pay closer attention to what was really going on inside of me. Thankfully, I chose the latter.

Looking inward helped me to see that it wasn't my children I didn't like; and it wasn't their childish behaviour I found so galling, either. It was the discomfort with how I was feeling during our interactions that I despised. Holding them responsible for how I was feeling was not only insufferable for me, it was unreasonable and unfair to them, and it was going to wear down our connection if I kept it up. This realization launched my commitment to check in with my heart before being led astray by the justification for my disdain my head so readily offered me. This new-found awareness precipitated a gradual shift inside of me and I slowly became more conscious of how I was feeling. In so doing, I became more patient when interacting with my rightfully immature children.

Here's what you can do...

If ever you find yourself thinking you don't particularly like your child, recognize that you're temporarily stuck in your head and that you need to check in with your heart. You're being flooded with frustration and it's dampening the caring feelings you have for your child. By acknowledging your frustration before it overwhelms you, you'll be empowered to see that it's not really your child you dislike, it's how you're feeling about yourself that you're reacting adversely to.

Today's parenting affirmation: I am willing to notice how I'm feeling inside.

10. I Need to Express All of My Emotions

BEING IN the presence of a distraught child is very unsettling for just about everyone. It either pulls out our caring instincts or it unnerves us and evokes our irritability. Either way, we want the distress to end. When young children are having an off day, it can be difficult to be compassionate about every little disappointment because there are usually so many. Once we begin to understand more about the value and importance of inviting their upset, regardless of how it appears, it becomes much easier to guide children through their emotions rather than trying to put a stop to them.

As parents, we've been entrusted with the responsibility of providing the conditions necessary for our children to feel and express all of their emotions. This is more than just an obligation, it's an honour to be the ones responsible for creating a safe space for our children to process their happy, sad, mad, and everything-in-between feelings. It doesn't necessarily always feel this way, but if we take the time to reflect on what we're being called to do, we find ourselves able to show more grace during our children's difficult moments.

When we commit to valuing and accepting all of their emotions, not just the pleasant ones, we naturally feel more confident and inspired to create the conditions needed by them to discover, explore, and process their deepest emotions without the risk of feeling shamed or disparaged during the experience. Supporting them to do this is not something we should ever take lightly or for granted.

In every interaction we get to choose: provide the room for children to express their thoughts and feelings openly with us, or attempt to change how they're feeling by trying to get them to see things our way. The latter is often more tempting as it puts us in a position of perceived control, and we feel like we're using the interaction to teach the child by helping them to see a situation differently. What's lacking in this flawed approach is the understanding that young children are not yet developmentally capable of considering our viewpoint at the same time they are holding on to their own. In these moments it's us who need a shift in perception, not them.

We must focus on allowing them to feel what they are feeling so they can begin to develop a relationship with their emotions and come to know themselves as creatures moved by emotion. Any time we shut down their feelings by dousing their expression with our logic, we lead them away from their hearts by trying to redirect them to their heads. Young children don't want or need to hear adult logic at this time. What they desire and deserve most is to be in the presence of a caring adult who acknowledges and validates what they are feeling. Most important, they need an adult who stays connected to them in a heartfelt way by resisting the temptation to suppress or judge their behaviour in their most vulnerable moments.

Any time we rush into reason with or admonish young children for getting upset, we're putting our need to quiet and control them ahead of their need to be heard. By doing so we unwittingly steer them away from learning to identify and trust their feelings, and we entice them to believe that uncomfortable emotions are bad and to be avoided, while pleasant emotions are good and more acceptable. Nothing could be further from the truth.

All emotions are equally valid and our capacity to feel them is what promotes emotional health. With time and maturity, expression of their emotions will become more controlled and they will no longer be as volatile, over the top, and dramatic. Our young children are relying on our support and understanding today in order to become emotionally mature adults in the future.

Here's what you can do...

Whenever possible, resist the temptation to try and reason your young child out of their upset state. When they are feeling sad or disappointed, know that it's because they are feeling the futility of what's not working. This is an uncomfortable experience, but it is natural and necessary for their emotional development. What they need is a caring parent who acknowledges their distress and guides them through, so they don't get stuck in it. Comforting a frustrated or upset child doesn't reinforce their "bad" behaviour; it allows them to feel taken care of and this supports their long-term emotional growth.

Today's parenting affirmation: I am capable of supporting my child through all of their emotions.

11. Don't Be Afraid of My Fear of Separation

WHEN IT comes to dropping off a young child at daycare or preschool, I've been on both sides of the fence. As the parent of a child who doesn't want you to leave, it's a heartbreaking and gut-wrenching experience. And as a preschool teacher, I've witnessed how extremely distressed and overwhelmed parents get when they're in this predicament. For both parents and teacher it can be agonizing to see a child distraught and not be able to make everything feel better.

I've also seen a wide range of children's reactions to being dropped off. Some children appear to show little or no angst about leaving their parents. They seem so confident and eager to get into the daycare or classroom that they barely look over their shoulders to call goodbye to the parents they've abandoned at the entrance. Others are like little limpets firmly affixed to the sides of their parents who seem to oscillate between sharing words of reassurance and expressing irritation fuelled by their concern and embarrassment. The common theme that stood out for me in these situations was the tendency for worried parents to try and reason with their unsure or overwhelmed children.

When parents get rattled by their children's fear they often panic and try and implement an approach that typically works on a mature brain. We list all the reasons they shouldn't be afraid and try and convince them to see our point of view rather than consider theirs. What we're inadvertently doing is giving them the message that they're misinterpreting how they're feeling. This isn't fair. They are alarmed, they know it, and they have every reason and right to feel this way. Although their seemingly over-the-top reaction to being left may not make logical sense to us, the fear is very real to them because they are experiencing a wave of powerful emotion.

A child who senses a threat, even if it is perceived rather than real, will move away from danger and toward security. Young children are wired to seek physical closeness with those to whom they are most deeply attached, and this is particularly appropriate when they feel unsure or frightened. There is nothing dysfunctional about that.

When circumstances dictate that we cannot be with our child, we must make sure that we foster connections between them and the adults who will take care of them in our absence. These people may include daycare providers, preschool teachers, program instructors, nannies, and family members. By expanding our young child's village of attachment we're making sure that when they are feeling insecure, they have caring adults to whom they can turn.

Once we're able to recognize and understand what's going on for a child who is resisting separation, we naturally begin to meet their need for more connection rather than trying to reason them out of their fearful behaviour. With the loving support of those they trust, young children come to see that they no longer need to fear separation as intensely as they once did, and with time and maturity they'll be able to wave us goodbye with a smile.

Here's what you can do...

When your child expresses fear or concern over you leaving, be sure to acknowledge their emotions as normal and natural. Giving them the sense that you like and trust the people who will take care of them in your absence is essential to them being able to settle. Always remember that your calm and confident presence is more helpful to a young child than your adult logic and reasoning will ever be.

Today's parenting affirmation: I am aware of the importance of keeping my emotions in check when I'm leaving my child.

12. Lots of Things Are a Big Deal to Me

· ·

WHEN MY children were young, there were many times our ordinary interactions would unexpectedly take a turn for the worse by morphing into what felt like unnecessary drama. Things would be going along peacefully when suddenly the calm would be shattered by a child who would take exception to something. Seemingly unimportant things like me giving my daughter a red cup instead of the blue one she'd hoped for, or me innocently suggesting she sit on the left side of the sofa when she was planning to sit on the right, would result in over-the-top reactions that made little sense to me.

In our adult world, a cup is a cup and any seat on the sofa is a perfect spot for me. As long as the object serves its purpose, we don't usually bother with the finer details, as we have other things to think about. To a young child almost everything is a big deal. When we don't understand what they perceive to be unfathomable, their animated objections let us know all about it. When my daughter lost her mind over the smallest things, I'd often get sucked right into her upset.

It's not uncommon for parents to get frustrated with a young child who seems to make a big deal out of nothing. As adults we have the benefit of life experience and perspective and we need to remember that for now, our young children have neither. To them, the little things really do matter because they lack the context to understand that in the big world, certain things really don't make much of a difference to the outcome. Unless we remember this when interacting with young children, we're likely to be triggered by their disproportionate reactions to what we already know to be inconsequential issues.

Given their current state of immaturity, young children really do believe their way is the only way. Their brains are not yet fully integrated, and so it does not cross their mind that we would think differently than they do. To them, they are right and when we make suggestions or do things that don't align with their outlook or expectations, they're quite taken aback and react indignantly. While giving them the incorrect colour of cup is an unintended oversight on our part, it is perceived as a very big deal to them and they can't help but act out in ways that let us know just how they are feeling.

While we cannot, and should not, try to predict every want and meet every whim of our children in an effort to appease them, it helps to keep in mind their disproportionate reactions to seemingly small issues aren't their fault—it's their current brain wiring. When we remember this, we're less inclined to lose our patience with them, and we're more likely to hold space for their immature reactions while they gather life experience and expand their perspective. As always, preserving our connection with them needs to be our top priority because that's what is most needed right now if they are to grow up to become mature, rational, self-controlled adults someday.

Here's what you can do...

Any time your young child makes a big deal out of something trivial remember that almost everything that doesn't go their way is a huge issue to them right now. Respond to their objection by acknowledging that they're upset and resist trying to subdue their reactions with adult logic and perspective. What they need most is to have you make room for their big feelings because they cannot see the situation any other way. They will someday, just not today.

Today's parenting affirmation: I am the best person to comfort my child through their upset.

13. My Shyness Isn't a Problem

NEITHER OF my young children were particularly eager to engage with strangers. When people would try and initiate contact with them, they'd tuck in behind me and resist peeking out, even if the friendly person persisted and tried to coax them out with promises of candy. I couldn't quite put my finger on why my children, who were so outgoing and interactive at home, would become like meek little mice who lost their tongues when we went out into the world.

I remember sometimes feeling a little embarrassed by their antisocial behaviour, particularly if their shyness peaked around people we already knew. It was one thing to avoid eye contact and clam up when spoken to by an unfamiliar cashier at the grocery store, but not wanting to greet family members had me somewhat concerned.

When I began looking into the science of attachment, the mystery of what was really going on for my shy children was revealed. Attachment theory says that if children are to survive, they need to attach to a caring adult whom they trust to take care of them and meet their needs. As long as children feel connected, and they can rest in an adult's care, they will have the secure base needed for healthy physical, emotional, and psychological development.

With this new insight, I realized I had misread my children's natural shyness as a deficit that needed to be overcome. It was actually an indication they were developmentally right on track. The inclination to withdraw from strangers, or those they haven't seen for a while, is instinctively wired into young children. Nature's way of keeping them close to those who love and protect them is to make them shy away from those who are unknown or unfamiliar. My children's shyness wasn't a problem; it was serving them well by keeping them close to me so they wouldn't be led astray by people outside their circle of close connections.

Once I understood this, I began to change my ways. Rather than putting them on the spot and insisting they engage with people, I took on the role of mediator. I gave up trying to get them to make eye contact and say thank you to the nice lady who had served us. Instead I thanked her from all of us. Once the pressure was off trying to get them to perform, things began to shift. I noticed my young children watched me closely as I engaged with people. If I seemed to like them and was enjoying a pleasant interaction, my daughters picked up on it and when we were ready to leave, they'd spontaneously wave and say goodbye as the stroller left the checkout. No prompting or persuading required, just being close to me and not feeling pressured to engage was all that was needed for them to warm up to the person behind the counter.

Nature's answer to overcoming shyness is connection and brain development. When children feel comfortable with those around them, they can't help but let their true selves shine. As they mature, they develop the capacity to have mixed thoughts and feelings. If conditions are conducive; they attach more deeply to the people who are consistently caring toward them. When brain integration and their sense of connection align, their shyness will naturally subside.

The instinct to be shy will always be present but if the child finds their own reasons for wanting to interact and their motivation to do so is bigger than their fear of engagement, they will find their true courage to speak to people or participate in activities they might otherwise have avoided. I've watched many preschoolers' confidence blossom as their attachment to me deepened and their desire to share their thoughts and ideas eclipsed their fear of being in the spotlight.

Shyness is completely natural, but in a world that sees it as a problem, it becomes treated as an obstacle to be overcome. Our calling as parents is to value and respect the presence of shyness in our young children. It is not a mistake that humans are born to be shy. We shouldn't feel embarrassed by its presence and we shouldn't be hasty to subdue it. As with all things we fear, inviting it into the light is the way through.

Here's what you can do...

Keep in mind that shyness is a self-preservation instinct and it's meant to keep your child close to you because you are their safe space. When they become bashful in the presence of strangers, family, or friends, don't draw their attention to it as this may evoke a sense of shame for how they're feeling. Draw them closer to you and take the lead in the interaction to help them warm up to the people you're hoping to invite into their circle of connection.

Today's parenting affirmation: I respect and appreciate my child's shyness as normal and natural.

14. Please Don't Resist My Tears

SELDOM DOES a day go by when young children don't shed any tears. They seem to have tears at the ready for all occasions. They cry when they are frustrated, disappointed, tired, unwell, scared, or sad. Very sensitive children may even shed tears when moved by a sight or sound that touches their heart deeply. All these tears can certainly wear down a parent's patience and when this happens, the words and actions that follow are likely to sabotage valuable opportunities that could be used to support the young child's emotional development.

Tears are meant to get our attention and illicit a caregiving response from us. However, if children's tears make us feel uncomfortable or inadequate, the very opposite may occur. Rather than evoking a caring response, their tears may provoke an angry or irritated reaction. While this is understandable, it's not helpful if our spontaneous reaction is to try and put a stop to the tears in order to alleviate the discomfort we're experiencing. By suppressing a child's tears, we're conveying to them their tears are not necessary or welcome. In so doing, we're leading them away from nature's intended purpose for tears, which is to promote the development of a healthy adaptive emotional system.*

By the time a child cries tears of sadness, loss, or disappointment, they have already experienced the emotional

---

* For more information about the adaptive process and how young children mature, see page 201.

hurt of things not going their way. When they burst into tears upon hearing they may not have another cookie, it's an indication they've felt the pang of futility associated with not getting what they so desperately want. Their tears are an external sign of their brain's acceptance of this very sad fact and shows they have entered the emotional process of adapting to circumstances they can't change or control. Contrary to what many parents think, tears do not signal that the emotional system is not functioning well; instead, they are the essential indicator that the child's healthy emotional development is taking place right before our eyes and their tears are meant to draw us in to comfort and console them.

Any time we shame, ignore, or punish a young child for crying, we're circumventing nature's brilliant process of brain adaption. A young child who is repeatedly dismissed or treated harshly for expressing their vulnerability will begin over time to suppress their feelings to try and stop their tears from coming. They may do so in an effort to stay in the good graces of parents who have a low tolerance for tears, or out of fear of repercussions that might follow their openly shedding tears. A young child who is less tearful may appear to be more resilient in the face of adversity, but this is a false front as true resilience requires an adaptive emotional system in order to bounce back. Their emotional hurt will still be present, but instead of being processed through tears of sadness, it may be expressed as aggression because the young child cannot release their frustration in a soft and vulnerable way.

Parents needn't worry that young children who are allowed to cry freely will someday become adults who cry whenever something doesn't go their way. Quite the opposite is true. A young child who is consistently nurtured through their upset will, over time, become more adaptable and resilient. Supportive conditions encourage the child's brain to integrate, and this will enable them to better access their mixed thoughts and feelings. A mature, well-integrated brain is what allows adults to process their feelings of sadness and disappointment without necessarily shedding tears on the outside, unless they feel safe and invited to do so. As parents, we are the ones who need to provide a safe space for our young children to have their tears so they will grow up to understand and honour their importance.

Here's what you can do...

When a young child sheds tears in your presence, they're looking to you to support them in their most vulnerable moments. Your willingness to comfort them when they are upset is what is most needed if they're to process their big feelings and adapt to what they can't change. By offering them your understanding and loving presence, you'll provide them with an invitation to rest in your care. You'll also create the conditions needed to encourage their healthy emotional growth and development.

Today's parenting affirmation: I can lovingly comfort my crying child without fear of spoiling them.

15. Focus on How to Be with Me (Not How to Control Me)

· ·

THERE ARE few situations as trying as being in the presence of a child who's behaving in ways that don't match up to our hopes and expectations. I have found myself in countless difficult interactions with many children. The discomfort I feel hasn't diminished, but my tendency to be sucked into what's going on most certainly has. It's not that I have figured out exactly *what to do* in these moments, it's more that I have found my way to being able to *be more present* with what is unfolding before me. That might sound like a lofty, rather Zen-like claim, but it's simpler to do than you might imagine.

When we approach any situation fuelled by the energy of wanting to control the child, we've already lost our way. I'm not suggesting we don't have a responsibility to stop them from destroying things or that we shouldn't keep them safe from harming themselves or others. I'm simply saying we need to be mindful of our actions, particularly when we're feeling panicked and pulled toward trying to control children. When we do, we inadvertently stray from what we are likely intending to do, which is to guide them through their behaviour and have them come out on the other side having learned from the experience and be better for it.

Although it can be tempting to do whatever we can to hastily bring a child back into line, each time we resort to using force or manipulation, we stray from the heartfelt intention to grow them into the caring and considerate people they are capable of becoming. Our focus should not be on scrambling to do something in the moment. Instead our aim should be to hold space for what is happening before us without becoming alarmed by what might happen if we fail to do something controlling or punitive to them.

Any time we find ourselves faced with a child who is struggling with themselves or against us, we must remember that our first priority is to be with them in their upset and not to join them in it. We don't need to fix what's not working, we don't have to make them feel better about it, all we need to do is *be* there for them so that we can make it easier for them to *feel* their pure emotion, as uncomfortable as it may be. Not being aware of our calling as parents to do this makes us more likely to try and suppress their emotions in order to make their unwanted behaviour stop. Attempting to do so will not serve their developing emotional system well, nor will it strengthen and deepen the connection we long to have with them.

Here's what you can do...

In your most trying parenting moments, make sure to take a few seconds to notice just how agitated you're feeling. Then turn your attention to your child. Allow yourself to observe their struggle. If you let your heart go out to them when they're upset, you'll feel yourself soften as you guide them through their powerful emotions. By being there with them, rather than trying to do something to them, you'll find what serves and supports them best during their most difficult times.

Today's parenting affirmation: I am willing to believe that gentle guidance is more effective than coercive control.

16. I Need to Trust in Your Comfort When I'm Scared

HAVING PARENTED two young children, I know first-hand what it feels like to be confronted by critics who misperceived my comforting them as overprotecting them. People were quick to point out that when my daughters were feeling unsure or afraid, they needed to be sent back in to face their fears so they would learn to get over them. The logic was that allowing my children to stay by my side would just reinforce their fearful behaviour. But this remnant of bygone parenting practices is misinformation. Sadly it continues to mislead loving parents who simply want to support their children's emotional development.

While we intuitively know that young children are wired to seek us out in times of distress, many parents feel conflicted about how to respond to a child who is driven toward us by their fear. Our heart tells us to scoop them up and make them feel safe, but our heads worry that we'll be rewarding their fearful behaviour and may risk preventing them from ever learning to manage their fear on their own. What is a parent to do? I have come to see that I needn't have worried about how to respond. I just needed to trust myself.

When my child is upset, my priority is to comfort them. Afterward, if need be, I can talk to them about their experience and help them make some sense of what was making them feel so afraid. It's never a matter of having to choose between giving comfort or teaching. We can do both because they are not mutually exclusive. In fact, they are most powerful when used in tandem.

Comforting a young child who is feeling alarmed typically requires physical closeness and gentle words. Readily picking them up and holding them close or inviting them to sit on our lap meets their need for tactile connection instantly. It's natural to use our words to calm them, and when we do, we should acknowledge their fears without using words or a tone that conveys any judgment for the way they're feeling or behaving. Validating their experience helps us to come on side with a child when they're emotionally distressed and helps settle their heightened emotional state.

Once the child calms down, we may be able to share a little reasoning with them, but we must be mindful of not launching into trying to convince them to see things our way. It's a dance that we figure out during the experience and some days our interactions will flow more easily than others. There's no prescribed formula and we must allow what we do to spontaneously unfold as we intuitively respond to our child's fearful behaviour. If we consistently honour our child's need for closeness and connection during their most vulnerable moments, they'll begin to rest in our care, and their brain will integrate, making it possible to someday face fear on their own with confidence and courage.

Here's what you can do...

When your child seeks your comfort in their moments of distress, take it as a compliment. It shows their attachment to you, and it conveys their willingness to share some of their most vulnerable emotions with you. By responding warmly to their need to be consoled, you're not only meeting their immediate need to be comforted, you're accepting their invitation to become one of the trusted people they'll continue to turn to for guidance and consolation as they grow older.

Today's parenting affirmation: I will lovingly offer my child comfort when they are distressed.

Caveat: Some young children don't appear to have a shy bone in their bodies. In a culture that admires independence and gregariousness, their lack of shyness may be misperceived as a strength rather than an early indication of a potential developmental concern. I have taught some young children who shy away from no one and appear to fear nothing. While this is the extreme, I encourage parents who have young children who appear to lack shyness or caution (when it's appropriately called for) to look a little deeper into what's going on for their child developmentally. Now is the best time to seek insight and support because these are the formative years that set the stage for their future.

17. Why I Battle Bedtime

. . . .

HAVING A conversation about tiredness with a person who doesn't have young children can feel like speaking to someone from another planet. Granted, everyone has their personal measure of fatigue relative to their own experience, but parents of young children know a special kind of tiredness. For me, the true meaning of exhaustion became clearer after I'd been in the sleep deprivation trenches with two children for a few years. Whenever I heard a childless adult (who got to choose when and how much they slept) complain about how exhausted they were, I had to bite my tongue so that I didn't launch into an "If-you-think-you're-tired-listen-to-my-story" tirade.

The designation of a "good sleeper" is given to children who go to sleep without a fuss and stay asleep until the adult deems their wake-up time to be acceptable. By this unfair definition, many children don't qualify as "good sleepers." Some need very little sleep and others struggle to stay asleep. A lack of sleep can make parents feel as though they're living on autopilot. I had my fair share of trial and error trying to figure out bedtime routines and how to manage the frequent nighttime calls. Things only started to get better once I understood more about why going to sleep, and sleeping alone, is so difficult for many young children and, more important, how my opposition to their resistance was making the situation worse.

From a child's perspective, bedtime is when the people they love most leave them to go off and do more important or exciting things. Even though we might not use these specific words, and the exciting thing we have to do is load the dishwasher, they pick up on our energy, which conveys our hurry to move the bedtime routine along. Children lock in on our intent to leave them like a shark senses blood in water. They become preoccupied with doing whatever it takes to keep us with them a bit longer, because they are emotionally agitated by the anticipation of the impending separation. There are few situations that draw out a lengthy list of last requests quite like a child who has been told that it is now time to go to sleep. Suddenly they are parched and are in critical need of a drink of water. They are famished and will surely die if they have to wait until the morning to have a snack. The urge to use the washroom escalates, and their creatively desperate requests rapidly multiply.

The more children resist going to sleep, the more desperate we seem to get, and bedtime preparations become a battleground rather than the buildup to a peaceful send-off to rest. Whenever we fixate on trying to get our children to go to sleep, we inadvertently make things more difficult on ourselves—and on them—than we need to. Yes, adult persistence may eventually appear to work, but when a child collapses out of sheer emotional exhaustion, few parents are left feeling satisfied. Relieved maybe, but seldom content with their methods.

I believe that intuitively we all know what drives a child who persistently resists going to sleep, but we're often so distracted by their constant requests and overt resistance that we misread what unfolds before us. We label their struggle as a bedtime behaviour problem that needs fixing rather than seeing the child as being innately moved to do whatever it will take to prolong their time of togetherness with us. Looking through this lens, we begin to see that what is most needed from us is not firmer discipline, nor a different sleep training technique, but instead, a shift in our focus.

We need to give more consideration to how they are feeling and focus less on what they are doing to delay the inevitable separation. When we generously provide them with more contact and closeness and stop drawing their attention to how many stories, minutes, or hugs they have left with us before we leave them, we're better able to fill them up with our presence rather than reminding them of our looming departure. If we change what we're paying attention to, we subtly shift the energy we bring to the bedtime experience. Instead, we find ways to emotionally settle our children and lead them into sleep. It's only then that we discover that bedtime doesn't have to be battle time.

Here's what you can do...

In the lead-up to bedtime, try and soften your actions that convey your intention to get your child to go to sleep. By establishing a routine that allows for more time to be spent connecting and enjoying your cozy time together, you'll be helping your child's emotional system to settle, which is essential to their being able to rest. Being generous with your presence, even when you're tired and have other things to do, will increase the chances of both you and your child having a more peaceful night.

Today's parenting affirmation: I will keep my focus on providing more connection and comfort at bedtime.

18. I'm Counting on You to Discipline Me

CHILDREN ARE counting on the adults in their lives to discipline them. Not to train or punish them into compliance, but instead to instruct or teach them as in the original Latin definition of the word *disciplina*. As parents we quickly discover that accepting the responsibility to teach our children right from wrong is the easy part. Figuring out how to do it is where the true challenge awaits.

Parents frequently ask me about the best way to discipline children. Many are confused by the myriad discipline approaches and don't quite know which advice is best to follow. Some feel tremendously conflicted because the most popular techniques are based on the premise that to teach children effectively, we need to make them suffer the consequences of their actions in some way. This unsettles parents as it requires them to disconnect from their hearts in order to implement a method which makes some sense to their head. When this happens, parents are typically led astray from their intuition and are left feeling disheartened and unsure of what to do.

After having my own children, I began to see that many caring parents were asking only a small part of a much bigger question. What they really wanted to know was, "What does my child need from me now in order to grow up and eventually become self-disciplined?" Seldom do parents articulate their question in this way because they are already in the trenches and want practical solutions ahead of insight. We don't want to waste any time and we put so much pressure on ourselves to find effective discipline strategies early on that we rush into implementing techniques without an awareness of the impact our actions may have on our young children's development and the relationship we are building with them.

This realization didn't dawn on me until a few years into my parenting journey. Like most new parents, I lived in survival mode. I had two children under the age of two and I stumbled around trying to figure out what worked and what didn't. Those first years were a blur, but thankfully I managed to shift my attention from only wanting solutions to also seeking insight. Once I backed off asking about what to do and started focusing more on what was going on developmentally for my children and between us relationally, a completely different path opened up.

With time I recognized that in my panic to discipline my children, I had overlooked that I already had the most important thing to teach them effectively: a strong and loving connection. My young daughters loved me and wanted to learn from me, and that was more empowering than any technique would ever be. They were naturally looking to me for guidance and direction. I didn't need to use contrived measures to discipline them, I simply needed to start seeing them as relational beings who longed to feel connected and naturally wanted to please me as they grew up.

Parenting is always going to include times when interactions get noisy, messy, and even unpleasant simply because humans don't like boundaries and limitations. Disciplining children requires them to feel the emotional discomfort of not having things go their way, and our calling is to hold them in this space without adding additional distress to drive our point home. If they are to adapt and grow and learn from their mistakes, we need to be conscious of our ways of disciplining. We need to make sure that we're holding boundaries firmly but kindly and are not resorting to punitive measures simply to try and control unwanted behaviour in the moment.

When we see our young children as needing our guidance rather than harshness, we come more into alignment with our heartfelt intentions to support them to grow into self-disciplined beings. This shift in perception leads us to seeking practices that will support us to discipline more effectively and most importantly, to nurture the relationship we'll need if we are to guide and teach our children as they grow.

Here's what you can do...

In moments when you feel yourself trying to manipulate your child into complying with your expectations, notice the gripping sensation that invades your body. When you're being driven by the urge to control your child, you're more likely to disconnect from your heartfelt intention to teach them. In this headspace you may resort to using contrived methods that sabotage their learning and your connection with them. Remember, what they need most is to have you respond to them in a firm but kind way without being distracted by their immature behaviour.

Today's parenting affirmation: I am open to gently guiding my child in order to teach them right from wrong.

19. How You Respond to Me Has More to Do with You Than Me

AS PARENTS we know that on some days we feel more on top of our parenting game than on others. It's understandable we would assume that our children's behaviour is what determines how we're feeling, because to some extent it does. When they are co-operative, our days are less intense and so we're likely to feel more competent and together. On other days, when they're cranky and defiant, we can't help but feel frustrated and worn out. There's no question that their behaviour impacts our mood, but, more often than we realize, it's our general underlying emotional state that sets the stage for how we respond to them.

Becoming more aware of my inner state has made an enormous difference in the quality of the interactions I have with my children. On days when I'm feeling content, everything seems to go better for us. It's not that everything works out for me the way I want it to, it's more that when things don't go my way, I'm better able to take it in stride and not become as provoked by them or the situation. Contrast this with days when I have a lot on my plate and I'm feeling overwhelmed or frustrated and it's a completely different scenario. I'm much more irritable and easily triggered and I'm far more prone to reacting without considering the potential impact of my words and actions. I have come to see that although my children's behaviour has an effect on the way I feel, they are not responsible for my behaviour. I am.

When I made a point of checking in with myself before engaging with my children, I came to notice that when I was feeling less stressed, even their most challenging behaviour wasn't such a big deal to me. Ordinary encounters like my repeatedly asking them to do something and them not doing it were still annoying, but rather than getting worked up over it, I'd simply remind them or help them to do what needed to be done. Sometimes I'd even just do it myself because it really wasn't necessary for me to call them on their every transgression. When I felt more relaxed within myself, I seemed to naturally align with what I needed to do and no longer felt the need to make mountains out of molehills. My children sensed my calmer disposition, too, and because I wasn't layering my pent-up frustration on top of theirs, we'd move through our day far more amicably.

My discovering this didn't take intellect; it took willingness and vulnerability. It required me to be open to seeing that the energy I was bringing to our interactions was having a direct impact on my relationship with my children and on our family. It's often much harder to look inward and consider our part in the equation than it is to look outside of ourselves and blame the actions of another for our conduct. When we consistently attribute our sense of inner discontent to the actions of our children, we tend to think it's them who need to change their behaviour, when really it's us who has the emotional work of adaptation to do.

Always keep in mind that young children are supposed to behave like immature children. Expecting otherwise is a recipe for parental disappointment. Children have their moments just like we do, and it's how we respond to them that predominantly influences how interactions between us unfold. As it turns out, how we behave when we are with them is something we can learn to control, but first we have to become aware of the impact of our ways and then be willing to change them if need be.

Here's what you can do...

When you find yourself being provoked by your child's behaviour, be sure to turn inward to get a sense of how you've been feeling lately. If you're able to recognize that you've been upset, stressed, or frustrated, you'll be more likely to stop yourself from making their current behaviour the reason for your acting out. How you are feeling determines how you behave and this has more to do with the buildup of frustration, hurt, or disappointment already in your emotional system than it does with what your child has done in this very moment. It's not always easy to do, but with a soft heart, a little willingness, and a bit of practice, you'll find your way.

If you are struggling with controlling your anger, consider seeking the support of a professional counsellor or therapist.

Today's parenting affirmation: I am willing to look at the energy I bring to my parent-child interactions.

20. Sending Me Away Doesn't Teach Me What You Hope

AS A parent, I have first-hand experience of the discomfort and inner dissonance that comes with trying to find the most effective way to bring a young child's wayward behaviour into line with my hopes and expectations. I know how it feels to be so desperate for answers that you're willing to try almost anything that might do the trick. Although at the time I couldn't pinpoint why certain approaches weren't working or why I felt so off in implementing them, the uneasiness in my gut let me know that it wasn't the way through.

Once I understood and respected that humans are driven by emotion, I began to get it. We're wired for connection and when we don't get the physical, emotional, or psychological closeness we need, we can't help but feel unsafe. When we feel insecure, we instinctively adapt our behaviour in an effort to draw those we love into closer connection with us. As young children, we had no choice but to depend on our parents to take care of us and so if it felt necessary, we changed our behaviour in an attempt to preserve or restore our connection with them. Our young children are moved to do exactly the same thing if they feel their belonging and security is contingent on being in our good graces.

Separation-based techniques, like the popular approach "time out," use what children care most about, against them. Knowing that a young child's greatest need is to be physically close to their primary attachments, it makes sense that separating them from their parents may get some children to change their behaviour, some of the time. The reaction of each child is predominantly influenced by their personal temperament, emotional sensitivity, and their depth of attachment to us.

Most young children comply because they're immature and need to be in our presence in order to feel secure. Others will co-operate because they want to please us, but, in our haste to send them to a time out, we don't always realize all they needed was a little more understanding and connection. Then there are those who resist with such intensity that we label them as strong-willed, and, despite our valiant efforts, they refuse to be manipulated into compliance. These are the children, I believe, who have been sent to wake us up.

Time outs can effectively manipulate the behaviour of some young children. Those who are generally easy-going and adaptable may appear to learn their lessons after a time out, but these same children would likely have changed their ways if they were calmly redirected without being sent away. Regrettably, young children who resist and push back against time outs are the least likely to benefit from the experience, but the most likely to be the recipients of this approach. By taking away the physical closeness they require, we inadvertently push them away emotionally in the moments they most need to feel a secure heart connection.

When we repeatedly resort to sending young children away from us, we risk overworking their emotional system and knocking out their desire to connect with us. When time outs no longer seem to "work," it's likely the child's feelings have been shut down because it hurts too much to tolerate being separated from those they love. This is no accident; this is the brain's attempt to protect the child from feeling the unbearable intensity of physical and emotional separation.

The notion of sending a young child into what they experience as physical and emotional solitary confinement is not only disturbing, it's illogical. Young children do not go off and think about the error of their ways, nor do they consider what they could do differently next time. Not because they intentionally refuse to, but because their immature brains are non-integrated and they are not yet capable of reflecting on their undesirable behaviour, least of all when they are flooded by feelings of alarm because they have been sent away.

Knowing that a child's greatest need is to be seen, heard, and valued by us, we can no longer in good conscience remove them from our presence under the guise of teaching them how to behave appropriately. Immature little beings cannot flourish in isolation and they cannot yet process their big emotions without our loving presence. They're counting on us to be there for them, especially in the moments when we're most tempted to send them away.

Here's what you can do...

When your child misbehaves or acts out inappropriately, remember they are most in need of guidance and not separation. Sending them away from you may change their behaviour, but it conveys the underlying message that in order to be seen and valued by you, they must conform to your expectations. Your ability to connect and advise them as they grow into their teen and adult years requires you to share a deep relationship, and to cultivate that, you need to nurture the connection you have with them when they are young.

Today's parenting affirmation: I'm willing to see my child as needing to be close to me—even when I'm most tempted to send them away.

21. This Is Why I Make a Mess

MANY PARENTS struggle with keeping ahead of the chaos left in their child's wake. It can feel like a full-time job just trying to keep the house in order when young children are in residence. They don't seem to notice the toys, clothing, and remnants of food they leave strewn across the household. Or, if they do, they don't seem to be bothered by the mess they make in the same way adults are. Constant untidiness can easily become a source of tremendous frustration for parents. When this happens, homes are often turned into battlefields.

Young children don't set out to make a mess. In fact, they aren't fully capable of planning ahead of time because their brains aren't yet sufficiently integrated. What this means is *they live in the moment*. The expression "go with the flow" applies very well to young children, as they go wherever their desires take them. One good idea leads to the next and before they know it, they have, in our opinion, made a mess or broken the rules. There have been many times when I've left my apparently occupied children unsupervised for just a few minutes and they've managed to turn an ordinary item like a marker or Play-Doh into a disaster situation.

It's only when we alert our child to the trail of their destruction that it dawns on them that they are the masterminds of the disarray that surrounds them! Whatever children are blissfully creating, experimenting with, or exploring becomes their entire focus. The resulting mess is an unanticipated by-product of the exploration, and our displeasure may leave them surprised and confused. After all, we're usually full of praise when they're quietly painting, but when they start venturing off the paper and onto the kitchen table and each other, we forget that this is a spontaneous progression from paper and our exasperated reaction makes this clear to them.

If we don't understand that children are not deliberate creators of disorder, we may react harshly to the evidence of their exploration rather than admire the pure force of curiosity from which it sprung. Our frustration may move us to admonish the child for the chaos, and we miss the opportunity to recognize the beauty of the innate creativity that fuelled it in the first place.

A child who is moved to explore and experiment is showing us they are filled with emergent* energy and are being driven from the inside to learn and discover. This is a developmentally desirable quality and it should be nurtured rather than suppressed. Of course, it would be irresponsible of us to allow them to destroy their surroundings in the name of development. Our job is twofold; first, to keep an eye on what's going on from an unobtrusive distance but still be close enough to intervene if need be. And second, if we miss the window for redirecting, it's up to us to manage our reactions to their happy accidents as best we can. We want to convey our appreciation of their exploration, but also let them know what the limits are. Finding our balance while surrounded by disarray is essential if we are to set limits while also keeping their spirit of curiosity alive.

---

* For more information about the emergent process and how young children mature, see page 200.

Here's what you can do...

When your child inadvertently makes a big mess, breaks something, or causes chaos, remember they didn't intend to. They're immature and can't yet think through the consequences of their actions. Respond calmly and correct them gently so that the lessons you want them to learn will sink in over time. They want to please you and to learn from you, but still have a lot of growing up to do and they need your understanding and help.

Today's parenting affirmation: I choose to see my children's mess as a reminder of their immaturity.

22. Your Worries About Me, Worry Me

WHENEVER I was worried about my young children, they were quick to pick up on it. Even when I intentionally tried to convey what I thought looked like a calm outer vibe, they intuitively sensed the uneasy energy within me, and our interactions were influenced accordingly. Young children watch us closely and read what we're communicating with our nonverbal actions. How we go about doing something speaks louder than our words, especially when we're being motivated out of concern for them.

The sort of worry I'm referring to here relates to the common concerns many parents share. It could be the fear that our child is struggling to part from us when being dropped off at daycare. It could be the concern we have for the child who can't yet use the toilet as independently as other children of the same age. It might even be the stress we feel around their inability to colour in pictures or cut out shapes quite as well as those we've seen on the display board at the preschool. Whatever the worry, there's a low hum of apprehension that buzzes around us when we're interacting with them, and their perceived "shortcoming" is at the forefront of our mind.

The energy that swirls around a parent desperate to get their child to do something they haven't yet accomplished is one of coercive encouragement. It conveys the underlying message that the young child is not good enough just as they are. As caring parents, we don't intentionally mean to come across this way but our preoccupation with getting our child to do what we think they should has the potential to make us more forceful and persistent than we ought to be.

When we worry, we tense up and unconsciously come at children with energy that conveys the message they're not matching up to expectations. Driven by our angst, we put our focus on trying to help them progress at a rate faster than they may be developmentally ready for. Our methods may become forceful, our words harsh, and our patience limited. Without an awareness of the underlying message we're unwittingly transmitting, we're at risk of inadvertently chipping away at their fragile confidence rather than supporting them to flourish as we had intended.

Young children who worry about not being good enough generally grow up to become adults who worry about the very same thing. Contrary to what some believe, being made to feel like we didn't measure up as young children does not readily translate into the resilience needed to persevere in the face of our inadequacies as we grow older. What does have the potential to inspire young children is having parents who believe in them and convey this to them in ways and words that are not tainted with the predominant energy of worry.

Becoming a parent who reflects back a young child's innate worth rather than projecting our worries onto them is well within our reach. With some awareness of how we're interacting with them when we're being consumed by worry, we're better positioned to shift our focus. We can then respect and appreciate their current abilities rather than fretting about how far they may still have to go.

Here's what you can do...

When you find yourself worrying about your child, notice the urgency you feel to do something to fix your fear. Rather than trying to predict the future implications of your concerns, draw yourself back into the present moment and remember that right now, your child is exactly who they are meant to be. When you meet them in this space, you'll be more aligned with supporting them in ways they need, rather than blindly barging ahead.

Today's parenting affirmation: I am open to worrying less and affirming my child's individuality more.

23. I Don't Want to Talk About It

AS ADULTS we've all experienced the discomfort of being spoken to when we don't feel like communicating. It may be that we find the topic uncomfortable or perhaps we don't want to hear what's being shared with us. It could even be that we're feeling disconnected from the person who is speaking, and we don't want to give our attention to them. Young children experience these same feelings and often we're the ones trying to converse with them when they aren't sufficiently open to hearing us. We need to recognize that.

When a child has made a mistake or acted in a way that we believe requires some discussion or correction, it's natural that we should feel a parental responsibility to bring it to their attention in order to guide them to change their ways. Our desire to do so sometimes leads us to approach them before we've considered their receptivity. When we bulldoze ahead without first trying to assess how they are feeling, we're at risk of inadvertently shutting them down so they can't take in our words. We need to be aware of that.

By being laser-focused on getting our message across, we tend to react with irritability instead of patience because we don't read their cues. We temporarily forget they are immature creatures of emotion and so our initial good-hearted attempt to help them becomes forceful and persistent and we inadvertently derail our heartfelt intentions. Trying to communicate with someone who won't listen is one thing, but when it's your own child who is resisting you, the intensity of your irritation is taken to a whole new level. Unless we recognize the feelings that are stirring up inside of us, we're likely to increase our forcefulness when what's really needed is a tactical retreat in the moment.

A young child who is feeling uncomfortable about their behaviour is typically being flooded by feelings of intense embarrassment, shame, or remorse. They might also be fearing the potential consequences that could follow their actions and as such, are not approachable at the time of the offending incident. Knowing this, we need to proceed with caution or our well-placed efforts to correct them could backfire and cause them to shut down further and resist us even more.

Some parents may feel conflicted about delaying the lessons they hope to impart. Although you might think the best time to teach a child is right after the transgression when it's still fresh in their mind, be aware that the situation will likely spiral from bad to worse. You'll forfeit the opportunity to get them to take in your words because the interaction becomes a battle.

A quick assessment of the young child's receptivity is always the place to start. Do your best to gauge their current state of openness before proceeding. If they spontaneously show feelings of sadness or remorse, comfort them and perhaps gently talk to them a little about how their actions have crossed the line. In contrast, if they are clearly overwhelmed, recognize that they are currently innately unreceptive to your efforts to correct them. Launching into a list of how they've failed to meet your expectations, or how they can improve their ways in the future, is wasted energy on your part and will work against your connection.

Opportunities to teach young children right from wrong are never in short supply, but it helps to get more adept at picking the best times to do so. Sometimes it's better to put a little time and space between the incident and our follow-up because this is what will make all the difference to them taking heed of our words. A child who feels understood and connected is a child who naturally soaks up what we share with them.

Here's what you can do...

Resist the urge to address every transgression in the moment. Not every action or behaviour requires an immediate conversation and those that do are often better had when a little time has passed and you're in a place of connection with your child. If they indicate they don't want to talk about it, they're not intentionally stonewalling you. They're currently being flooded by their emotions, and they don't have the capacity to take in the lessons you want to teach. There will always be tomorrow and the day after that.

Today's parenting affirmation: I will use kind words because they open my child's ears and speak to their heart.

24. I Don't Only Want to Play, I *Need* to Play

....

WHEN PARENTS pick up their young children from pre-school or classes, many can't resist inquisitively asking what their child did during their time there. They are typically given a stock answer, which may include the words, "Nothing," or, at best, "I just played!" Neither of these usually satisfy parents eager to hear their child's time was used productively and has contributed to their acquisition of new skills and knowledge. For many parents, serious learning is the point of sending children to organized facilities and to hear their child didn't experience it as such can be disappointing.

What some parents don't always realize is young children learn best through play! When a child gets to play, they naturally learn because they are having fun. It doesn't occur to a young child that learning is a desirable outcome of their enjoyment—and that's a very good thing. They simply play for the sake of playing. The minute we alert them to having to meet certain criteria or work through a specified curriculum, we dampen their innate desire to learn for the enjoyment of the experience and instead make it about meeting contrived milestones and goals they were previously oblivious to. The minute they're expected to work rather than play, their joy and enthusiasm is sucked out of the experience. A developing brain needs plenty of unstructured opportunity to freely explore the environment and discover things for itself.

When a young child's tummy is filled up with food and their hearts are sufficiently satiated with feelings of closeness and connection to their primary caretakers, they're spontaneously moved to play. Their developing brain senses when their physical and emotional needs have been met and when this happens, all that's left to do is to play. Young children don't need structured activities or formal lessons because they're naturally wired to learn best through the processes of exploration, discovery, and creativity. A child who is curious, interested, and eager to learn is this way because their growing brain is primed and ready to take in new information. We must not get in their way with our adult attempts to channel their learning in an effort to meet our expectations.

Bursts of energy that fuel explorative play do not usually last very long for young children. Just as a snack doesn't fill them up for hours, their hearts don't remain topped up with feelings of closeness and connection indefinitely. Staying close by, but not interfering in their play, is just what young children need from us as they begin to explore and immerse themselves in play for increasing stretches of time. We can be sure that when they start seeking us out it's because their tummies or hearts, or both, need replenishing. Knowing this we can provide them with what they need most and we'll be less likely to be tempted into thinking they simply need to be given suggestions of things to go off and do.

There are many different types of play. Some play serves the purpose of cognitive enrichment. During this play young children discover skills that will later be required of them in the formal learning environment. For now, they'll get this through plenty of hands-on experience. Playing with something like wooden blocks introduces them to abstract concepts such as sequencing, mass, and the effects of gravity, but young children don't need to be told this. Their active participation is the doorway to learning all about it first-hand.

Figuring out what works and what doesn't puts them into the driver's seat of their own learning. Having to rebuild a tower that keeps falling over introduces them to the laws of physics, but more important, it allows them to experience the process of frustration, which is essential to their emotional growth. Finding their own reasons to get that tower of blocks to stand tall is how they discover their capacity to persevere in the face of difficulty and it's an attribute we could never teach them directly. The beauty of play is it teaches young children more than we could ever hope to.

Pretend or make-believe play invites young children to process their everyday experiences and allows them to face their deepest fears. When they immerse themselves in an imaginary world of their making, it frees them up to access and express their most vulnerable feelings and inner worries because in this realm, nothing is for real. They're able to dip into emotions that might overwhelm them in reality. By pretending they get lost in the mall they access their fear and sadness of what that experience might be like for them. Because it's not for real they're able to access their vulnerable emotions and indirectly experience feelings that would otherwise be too unbearable to tolerate.

By playing through their fears, young children process their feelings rather than avoiding them. In this way, play not only provides a safe space for young children to experience the unthinkable, it also gives parents a window into their children's inner world. By carefully watching them without being intrusive, parents can garner deeper insight into what young children may be struggling with and this empowers us to support them as they grow.

Here's what you can do...

Play is not a waste of time. Every minute a child spends immersed in creative, expressive play they're building the brain they will one day use at school and at work. Instead of putting your focus on trying to get your child to play, make sure you're providing them with lots of contact and closeness and plenty of time to play. When they feel filled up, they'll naturally want to explore and create. You can't make them play, but you can help make it possible for them to want to.

Today's parenting affirmation: I appreciate and prioritize the role of play in my child's healthy development.

25. When I Help You, I Feel Important

∙∙∙

SOME OF my fondest (and most frustrating) memories of my young daughters revolve around having them help me with household chores and other tasks on my to-do list. It amused me to see how eager they were to tackle tasks, especially ones I didn't find particularly engaging or pleasant. They were keen volunteers when it came to peeling vegetables, raking leaves, sweeping floors, and even cleaning toilet bowls. Their willingness to help me became an opportunity for us to do ordinary things together and I'm happy to share they now recall some of these times as being pleasant childhood events.

It can sometimes be difficult to get parents to entertain the idea of inviting young children to do household chores with them. When we approach our lives with a time-scarcity mindset, we automatically rule out asking children to participate simply because speed and quality work feature very high on our priority list. We think it will be quicker and easier to just do it ourselves, and we'd probably be correct, but by excluding our young children we miss out on opportunities to convey to them the important message that their presence and contributions are valued by us. If we are aware of these seemingly insignificant but powerful openings in our ordinary day-to-day activities, we're led to connect with our children without having to schedule it in or to feel bad about not being with them because we're so busy cleaning the house.

Inviting young children to participate in chores shouldn't be done to teach them life skills or lessons in perseverance. If that naturally happens, it will be a welcome by-product. When we make teaching the focus, it dilutes the message we want to send, which is that we welcome their presence and appreciate their help. Accept ahead of time that their initial enthusiasm will not readily translate into them sticking around until the job is done. By understanding their efforts are unlikely to result in a perfect job done, we'll avoid tainting the interaction with our disappointment or frustration because they didn't finish the job to our satisfaction.

By appreciating their interest and willingness to assist us, we'll be led to notice and perhaps even reclaim some of the joy to be found in the everyday and mundane tasks that have to get done. Our patience will be tested and tolerance for their less-than-perfect contributions will be stretched, but by inviting them to help us out we'll be nurturing the connection we share in even the most ordinary moments.

Here's what you can do...

By inviting your child to help you with everyday tasks you'll convey to them that you value and appreciate their presence. In so doing, you'll be instilling in them a sense of purpose and belonging. Just like us, they long to feel they matter and are contributing in some way. By putting your focus on including them rather than on the quality of the job they're doing, you'll be making the most of ordinary interactions and fostering a deeper connection between the two of you. You'll also get the chores done, which you would have had to do anyway.

Today's parenting affirmation: I will invite my child to help me more often so they feel seen and valued.

26. I Don't Want You!

I'LL NEVER forget the searing rejection I felt when I walked into my young daughter's room and was met with a scowl and the sharp words, "NO, want Daddy!" I was taken aback by her brashness and lack of enthusiasm upon seeing me. I didn't know how to respond and before I said a word, she upped her protest and began screaming, "Go away!"

My sweet little girl, who up until this moment was typically delighted by my presence, was clearly no longer feeling the same way. To add insult to injury, her father came bounding into the room upon hearing he had been summoned. He seemed oblivious to my anguish and appeared quite thrilled to learn he had finally displaced me to become our daughter's favourite person!

I realize now I was taking the whole situation far more personally than I should have. What felt like a personal slight, really wasn't. My daughter's rejection was not only natural, it deserved to be celebrated as an indication of her readiness to expand her village of trusted adults. But I didn't know that back then.

Whenever the inconsiderate behaviour of the immature child distracts us from seeing what's really going on for them, we accidentally misread their rejection as being personal. It may trigger unconscious inner wounds. If this happens, we risk reacting in ways that sabotage rather than promote the developmental process that's unfolding before us. Knowing that young children can't yet connect emotionally to more than one person at a time empowers us to understand their choosing someone else over us at this tender age isn't an intentional or manipulative attempt to hurt our feelings. It's where they are currently at developmentally and it's not their fault.

As young children become more deeply attached to their primary caregivers, they naturally want to keep them all to themselves. Most often, mothers appear to be the first chosen ones in their babies' and toddlers' lives simply because they are more physically present, but this may vary depending on the circumstances.

As the young child becomes more secure in their attachment to their favourite person, they feel moved to explore their connections with others. When my daughter chose her father's presence over mine, it wasn't at the expense of her relationship with me, it was in addition to her connection to me because she felt secure with me. Her early positive attachment experience had successfully laid the foundation needed for her to want to explore her connections with others, which opened the possibility of inviting them into her expanding circle of trusted people.

As parents we needn't worry about being permanently ousted from our young child's preferential person top spot. They will naturally begin to flip-flop their attention and affection between us and a few close others. Our focus needs to remain firmly on deepening the connection we have with them and making sure that we better understand their ways. By consistently being a loving and trusting presence, even when we're feeling sidelined, we're positioning ourselves as their home base and they will continue to orient toward us even as they grow up and venture further into the world.

....

Here's what you can do...

When the day arrives and your young child chooses another dependable person's presence over yours, remind yourself their doing so is an indication of their attachment development being on track. As best you can, resist feeling rejected and pushed aside. Instead, welcome it as an opportunity to share the caregiving responsibility with the one who has been called upon. You will soon be back in favour as young children cannot help but oscillate between the people they are deepening their relationships with.

....

Today's parenting affirmation: I welcome the additional support that comes along with my child's expanding circle of attachment.

27. I'm Just Doing It for Attention

IF EVER you've suspected your young child was just doing something to get your attention, you'd be absolutely correct! It's completely normal and natural for young children to want to be the centre of their loved one's attention. Newborns arrive instinctively knowing that gurgling and crying attracts people to them. Their crying helps ensure adults will meet their needs during their most vulnerable early months. After all, without our attention and caregiving they wouldn't survive.

Infants are typically willing to be held, consoled, and fed by anyone who offers closeness and nourishment. Some new parents feel a little put out by this during their early parenting days. Although we like to think our babies prefer being cared for by us, for many babies, anyone holding the bottle and willing to rock them will do. This naturally begins to change as they develop because they start to form a deeper connection with their consistent caregivers. They learn to trust specific people and this early experience becomes the foundation on which they build their future relationships.

Babies soon learn that in addition to crying, being cute and adorable also draws their parents in and they delight in the warm connection that follows. With time, they may share some of these endearing behaviours with others because they figure out this garners them more care and attention. This behaviour isn't premeditated or manipulative; it's nature's way of ensuring they are noticed and taken care of by those around them.

As babies grow into toddlers and then into young children, they become more verbal and independent. Although they are capable of doing many more things for themselves, their need to *feel* taken care of remains just as strong. Some parents start to back off some of their caregiving duties when children are as young as two or three years old as they notice their young children becoming more capable. Many consider the first signs of children managing on their own to be a limited window of opportunity to teach them to take care of themselves and in so doing, may push rather than gently encourage true independence.

When we put children in charge of too much of their own caretaking early on, some young children may misperceive this as a lack of attention. Given that all young children have an innate drive to be taken care of, they need to feel noticed in order to feel connected and so they are instinctively driven to attract attention to themselves. If they do not feel that their physical and emotional needs are being adequately met, they start seeking attention in more creative and persistent ways. Unfortunately, the behaviours that may have served them well when they were just a bit younger no longer yield the same considerate responses from parents. Their efforts may backfire on them because parents misinterpret their children's motives and therefore resist them, leaving the young child feeling confused and rejected.

There's a lot going on emotionally for a child who repeatedly acts out to get a reaction from their parents. Any time a young child ups their performance and becomes louder, more dramatic, or repeatedly pushes the limits, they need *more* attention, *not* less. This may sound contrary to what you've been led to believe, but withholding attention from a child who is acting out to get it will never resolve what's driving them to act out. When we ignore, shame, or punish a child who is "just looking for attention," we might succeed in temporarily shutting down their acting out, but we miss out on giving them what they truly need from us: a deeper heartfelt connection.

For a young child who is desperate for a parent's attention, even negative attention is better than not getting any attention at all. It's a poor substitute for the warm connection they were trying to attract, but they'll settle for what they can get. Parents need to know that the young child isn't going to be the one to break the cycle of acting out in order to get attention, it has to be the parent. We have to be the ones who let go of trying to justify how much time and attention we're already giving them, and thinking that it should be enough. Only the child knows how much is enough for them. If we're seeing their behaviour escalate, we have to approach their exasperating behaviour as an immature plea for more connection, not less, because that's what it is.

Here's what you can do...

Whenever your child appears to be doing something for attention, it's because attention is exactly what they need. When you push back or try and ignore their efforts to get your attention, you're wasting an opportunity to give them the connection they are seeking. By giving them loving attention, you're not giving in or letting them have their way—you're communicating that you see them, hear them, and they matter to you. This provides the necessary context to convey that no matter what their behaviour, your connection to them remains strong.

Today's parenting affirmation: I choose to see my child's attention-seeking behaviours as a plea for more connection.

28. Sometimes I Cry Many Tears Over Little Things

AS HEARTBREAKING as it can be for a parent to see their young child crying, parental compassion can quickly turn to irritation when children seem to cry at the drop of a hat. Many adults have been raised to believe that tears should be saved up and only shed over the really big futilities in life, like a devastating catastrophe or the loss of a loved one. Sayings like, "There's no point in crying over spilled milk," and "Don't give me those crocodile tears," not only devalue the purpose of tears, they also leave the tearful child feeling ashamed for expressing their vulnerability. Unless we shift this perspective, we'll inadvertently lead our children into a future where they suppress their tears at the expense of their developing emotional system.

Young children have a lot to cry about. On any given day, more things don't go their way than do and this leads to a lot of frustration building up in their emotional system. This frustration needs to be released, and one of the ways humans discharge it is by having their tears of sadness. When young children feel the sadness and disappointment in what they can't change, can't do, or can't have, they should be moved to cry about it. When they are able to have their tears in the presence of a caring parent, their brain recalibrates and brings them to rest as they accept what can't or won't work for them.

Young children who have been repeatedly shamed or punished for having their tears may stop crying in order to avoid the repercussions of their actions. Although it may appear as though they have better control over their emotions, what they have likely done is suppress their caring feelings. If they don't care, they don't feel their sadness, and they won't feel moved to cry. It's that simple. If this happens, children unconsciously find alternative ways to express their frustration and may become increasingly aggressive toward others, things, or themselves. When a child stops crying because they don't feel safe or supported to do so, their substitute behaviour will likely give us plenty to worry about.

Making it easy for young children to have their tears with us is one of the most beneficial gestures a parent can make. Every time a child is moved to tears and we can be there for them in a supportive rather than dismissive way, we're paving the path for them to become more adaptive and resilient. The seemingly silly things children cry about are often the gateways to invite them to have their tears with us. By not trivializing their loud and dramatic outbursts when they trip and fall, or by resisting the urge to tell them off for wailing like it's the end of the world because the cookies are finished, we're guiding them toward being able to share the bigger upsets that will inevitably come their way as they grow older.

Here's what you can do...

When your child cries over seemingly insignificant issues, be willing to invite their tears without judgment and try not to reason them out of their sadness. By acknowledging that they're upset, you'll be nurturing their vulnerability and helping them to process their frustration in a natural and healthy way. This is exactly what's needed if they're to grow into caring, compassionate adults who feel their sadness rather than acting out destructively because of it.

Today's parenting affirmation: I will comfort my child through their tears as this supports their healthy emotional development.

29. Counting 1-2-3 Isn't Magic

ONE OF the most common strategies parents use to get co-operation from their children is to count 1-2-3 to them. Who hasn't tried this method? When your child isn't complying and you're annoyed, you say, "I'm going to count to three, and if you don't stop what you're doing by the time I get to three, you're in big trouble." You say the number one in a warning voice that indicates your disapproval of their conduct. If they don't change their behaviour for the better, you up it to number two using a more assertive tone. If that still doesn't do the trick, you count to number three and then, that's it—no more chances. The young child now typically has to face an unpleasant consequence of your making. And, as the parent, you feel somewhat obligated to serve them with one in order to make your stance known and to communicate that you mean business.

This approach assumes that a young child has the maturity to consider the consequences of their actions and reflect on their wrongful ways in the moment. The fact is, they are not developmentally capable of doing either as their brain is not yet mature enough to do so. Making a choice is difficult at the best of times, and it's almost impossible—even for adults—to make a choice under stress. Reflection requires brain integration and maturation and takes many years of conducive conditions to develop. Unless we know this, we'll blindly resort to using 1-2-3 as a quick-fix discipline technique in order to frighten children into temporary compliance.

Scaring children with the threat of looming consequences may result in a temporary halt in their undesirable behaviour, but it does not ensure they will learn from the experience. If they did, they wouldn't do what young children typically do, which is to repeat their same mistakes a few times over. For a young child to learn from us they need to be open to taking in what we want them to know, but they can't do this effectively when they are under duress. Not understanding this leads many well-meaning parents to use disciplinary measures that work against what they are trying to do, which is to guide and to teach their child.

As a frustrated mother of two young girls, I borrowed a library book claiming to be the magic steps required to transform resistant children into obedient minions. How tempting does that sound to a parent wanting a quick and easy solution? What I had been doing was mostly working before I picked up that book, but I had become tired and impatient and wanted a speedier method requiring less of my energy while yielding more instant results.

My first few attempts at implementing this magic approach on my young daughters resulted in them being very confused. They were quite puzzled as to why I was randomly counting when I had previously always explained what was expected of them before guiding them toward doing it. After a few goes, they seemed to catch on. If my eyes got bigger and my voice got deeper and I started counting in s-l-o-w m-o-t-i-o-n, they knew something unpleasant was about to take place.

For a while they jumped through my hoops out of fear and confusion. Although it made little sense to them that my spontaneous counting was directly related to their lack of cooperation, they didn't like how I behaved after counting. Despite this, I remember thinking this approach seemed to be somewhat effective because they'd sometimes do what I insisted but something about interacting with them in this way still didn't sit well with me. Yet, if so many other parents were using this technique, and it reportedly "worked" for them, what harm could I possibly be doing?

The evidence of harm became apparent in just a few days, the technique was losing its effectiveness and my children appeared to be losing their hearing. I'd not be getting my way and I'd launch it to a prolonged *onnnn-nnne*. They wouldn't even look up. I'd move into a more forceful *twooooooooo*. Still nothing. I'd inwardly start questioning where all this was going and find myself adding in *twooo-and-a-haaaaaalf*. I'd see a spark of attention as they tried to figure out where this was leading. I'd keep going, *two-and-three-quarterssssssss*. Nope. Nothing. That's it then, THREE.

I came to see that delaying my arrival at three was my gut telling me this wasn't where I wanted to go. I intuitively knew that I didn't want to parent forcefully and that giving my young children consequences wasn't teaching them what I wanted them to learn. I was trying to scare them into doing what I wanted. It felt so wrong and having to figure out what I was going to do to make them suffer for their noncompliance felt archaic and contrived. It felt like me against them, and I was losing. I was losing them. My frustration was at an all-time high and their will to listen to me was at an all-time low. Something had to change, and it had to be me.

I gave up trying to use a technique that didn't feel right to me. I returned that library book out of obligation, but to this day it doesn't sit well with me that my doing so has resulted in other desperate parents getting their hands on it. I hope that those who will read it will see what I saw. The technique didn't not work because I was implementing it incorrectly. It wasn't working for me because it was eroding what I was wanting to have with my children: a long-term relationship built on mutual love and respect rather than fear and retribution.

Here's what you can do...

When you feel yourself scrambling to use a control technique on your child in order to procure compliance rather than co-operation, notice if the feeling of frustration, discontent, and disempowerment wells up inside of you. Remember that force and punishment may result in fearful obedience, but it isn't going to foster willing co-operation. Connection ahead of control is slower and requires more of your patience and presence, but it's also more in alignment with who you truly are and will be more effective in the long term.

Today's parenting affirmation: I am open to considering that quick-fix discipline does more harm than good.

30. You Can't Make Me Feel Sorry

IF YOU'VE ever visited a playground, the chances are you've witnessed a young child tossing a handful of sand directly into the face of another. As the parent of the child on the receiving end, a wave of irritation, upset, and desire to set the little perpetrator straight probably crashed over you. As the parent of the young child who broke the golden rule of sand play, you'll relate all too well to the feelings of distress and agonizing embarrassment that accompany those who feel responsible for the behaviour of a young child.

Regardless of which side of the sandstorm parents are on, all parties are looking to see if the young child who acted inconsiderately shows any remorse for their actions. As parents we can't help but worry when we don't see even a glimmer of regret, because deep down, we fret that unless we do, we might be in the presence of a budding sociopath. Not many parents voice that aloud, but I think it crosses most caring parents' minds at some point.

More often than not, the look on a young child's face immediately after launching sand in the direction of another is pure astonishment. Some even find humour in what they have just done. It's as though they hadn't predicted the impact of their actions or anticipated the objections that would follow. The fact is, their immaturity is predominantly what prevents them from thinking through the consequences of their gritty offences. Their currently non-integrated brain isn't capable of focusing on what they are doing and predicting potential consequences of their actions at the very same time.

When we understand that young children are currently developmentally inconsiderate and impulsive, we begin to tame our reactions to their transgressions. Keeping our focus on preserving their dignity in the moments they have wronged another should be at the forefront of our minds. All too often we launch into pointing out the error of their ways and the impact they've had on another when it hasn't even registered for them that they are the creators of the chaos. Parents are quick to deconstruct the wrongdoing and then move to eliciting an apology from the child who has not yet made sense of the situation. Parents need to s-l-o-w d-o-w-n.

We can and must show children how to give an apology, *but* insisting that a child do this in the heat of the moment often provokes shame around their immature behaviour instead of evoking feelings of heartfelt remorse for their actions. Putting a young child in the position of having to give an apology before being able to move on with their day is inadvertently working against what we're hoping to teach them.

Parents can't force children to feel sorry, but we can make it safe for them to feel their sorrow. By maintaining a safe emotional space free of blame and shame, we're laying the foundations necessary for the child to be able to feel their vulnerability so they can access feelings of true remorse for their actions. Keep in mind that young children are not yet developmentally capable of feeling bad for another at the very same time they are feeling bad for themselves. Demanding an apology might extract "I'm sorry," but if the feeling of remorse isn't connected to it, the words are hollow.

Teaching children how to *say sorry* is very different from trying to make them *feel sorry* for their actions. As parents, we are in the prime position to model giving apologies because young children are constantly watching and learning from us. They need to know that everyone, even adults, sometimes make mistakes. Even more important, through modelling we're empowered to take the lead in situations where it is socially expected that an apology be given by our young child. Many heated exchanges have been sparked in playgrounds when parents feel their child has been further wronged by not receiving an apology from the little perpetrator. Parents of the so-called troublemaker can make the most of this situation by stepping in to give an apology on behalf of their child. This not only settles the disgruntled parent down; it makes amends with the recipient of the flying sand and it gives all parties the opportunity to experience the power of a genuine, heartfelt apology.

We can follow this same practice in our homes when settling disputes between siblings. Rather than forcefully insisting that hollow apologies be muttered under their breath before they can return to what they were doing, ask directly if the child has a sorry inside of them and if they'd like to give it away. If not, move on. Apologizing on their behalf and gently suggesting that if they feel sorry later on, they can always share it then. Prolonging battles for the sake of getting children to say the word "sorry" is a waste of energy and defeats the purpose of a genuine apology.

Our focus needs to stay on making it safe and easy for children to access their feelings. If they can count on us to support them to have their feelings rather than having us try to shape their behaviour to act as if they are experiencing their caring feelings, with time and development they will freely give heartfelt apologies. They'll do so because they want to rather than because they have to. It may take a while, but when it happens, being in the presence of a young child who gives a sincere apology is always worth the wait.

Here's what you can do...

When your young child wrongs you or another in some way, keep in mind they are immature little beings who do not yet consider the implications of their actions ahead of time. Remember that making them regret their actions by shaming them is very different from inviting them to feel safe enough to access the vulnerability required to feel remorseful for their actions. A heartfelt sorry cannot be forced or hurried along and so we need to support young children during the process and be patient with them as they learn and grow.

Today's parenting affirmation: I can model heartfelt apologies instead of forcefully insisting my child give one.

31. Boys Need to Cry, Too

ASK ANY little boy in the midst of his tears if he *needs* to cry, and the answer will always be a heartfelt "yes." Ask him if he is *allowed* to cry and the answer will, in far too many cases, be a sorrowful "no." The antiquated fallacy that boys don't need to have their tears in the same way girls do has been passed down through generations and it's derailing the healthy emotional development of many boys during their early years.

Parents who are hoping to toughen up their sons to fit into a society that venerates men exhibiting toughness are neither ill-intentioned nor malicious. They have been misled by a false but prevailing belief that boys shouldn't cry. Some beliefs are hard to change, and this is certainly one of them.

When we consider that boys and girls have the very same emotional systems, it's mind-boggling to think they would need to be treated differently. Being able to feel their sadness is what moves young children to have their tears. Tears are meant to signal to us they're upset and in need of our comfort. Intuitively we may be sensing this, but the misplaced good intention to protect them from someday becoming men who are considered to be wimps or too soft, sometimes moves adults to respond in unhelpful ways.

Common parental reactions include frequently trying to talk boys out of having their tears or consistently shaming them for having them. When we unconsciously resort to using phrases we may have heard ourselves growing up, we say things like, "There's no need to cry," or "Big boys don't cry." By doing so we're plugging their tears, numbing their vulnerability, and inadvertently trapping their sadness inside of them. This works against what nature is trying to do, which is to move sadness out of the upset child and into the hands of caring parents who are ready to wipe their tears and comfort them lovingly.

Boys who from a young age are encouraged to share their tears and emotions will naturally grow into men who feel their vulnerability and express themselves in socially acceptable ways. Nature wires their mature brains in such a way that they have self-control and do not need to physically act out on their frustration or burst into tears whenever they feel moved by powerful emotions. This is because they're able to *feel* their emotions. Rather than suppressing or acting out on them, they learn to process them and find healthy ways to express themselves. Knowing this, there's no reason for us to fear the tears of our boys or cling to the misguided belief that tears are unmanly. Once we understand tears, we're able to do better for our crying boys, and they're counting on us to do just that.

Here's what you can do...

When your son cries, do all you can to invite his tears and be there for him in his time of need. By trusting you with his tears he is showing great vulnerability, and this should never be used against him. What he needs most is to feel safe enough to have his tears so that he can keep finding them as he grows into a caring, compassionate, wholehearted man. Always remember that right now, there's no one better positioned than you to do this for him.

Today's parenting affirmation: I am honoured to be the one who comforts my son through his tears.

32. Why I Lie to You

. . . .

DISCOVERING A sticky-faced child surrounded by a collection of empty candy wrappers is a scene that eventually plays out in most households. Although what has taken place is abundantly clear, when the young child is directly questioned about what they have done, the story that follows doesn't seem to match the evidence. Parents find themselves scrambling to respond as they fear that unless they act swiftly to stamp out deceitful behaviour, their children could potentially grow up to become compulsive liars.

It's unsettling and infuriating for a parent to have their young child look them in the eye and deny they had anything to do with what has taken place. It can be difficult to know how to manage a situation and correct the behaviour of a child who adamantly denies their participation in the wrongdoing. In their confusion, parents often react in a harsh, knee-jerk manner because they don't quite understand what they're dealing with. Their fear-driven retaliation often results in a harsh reaction intended to stop the child from ever lying again, but there is a more gentle and effective way through.

Take comfort in knowing that a young child who has the capacity to tell a lie is developmentally right on track. Although lying *is* considered to be socially and morally unacceptable by adults, it is developmentally appropriate for young children. Before the age of around five years old, young children really do believe many of their own lies. Because their immature brain is not yet able to hold two thoughts simultaneously, the dominant thought of that moment is the one they put forward as their truth. They really do believe it wasn't them who gobbled up the forbidden candy and we can't convince them otherwise.

At around the age of five or six, the young child's brain begins to integrate. Their capacity to consider the consequences of their actions increases, and they may begin to tell lies whenever circumstances deem it to be in their best interests. Once they discover that telling a convincing lie can keep them from getting into trouble, it makes perfect sense to lie. They also cue into lying being a sure-fire way to remain in the good graces of their parent. To the young child, if Mommy or Daddy isn't disappointed in or mad at them, then their relationship isn't threatened. To the immature child, these are compelling reasons to tell a barefaced lie.

With this insight in mind, our focus needs to shift away from trying to harshly crack down on lying when they are young. While shaming and punishing children for lying may certainly appear to work in the short term, over time we're inadvertently pushing them toward sneakiness and secrets, which will inevitably make it more difficult for us to guide them as they grow.

Alternatively, by making children feel safe early on in their relationship with us, they naturally move into more readily telling us the ugly truth instead of fabricating a pretty lie. Perhaps not all of the time, but certainly more of the time. Telling the truth becomes easier when they do not have to fear being shamed or punished for admitting their mistakes and revealing their shortcomings. They tell the truth because it feels uncomfortable and disingenuous to deceive those they love and trust. With time and maturity, being honest leads them to developing a sense of personal integrity, and this will guide and serve them well in their future adult relationships.

Here's what you can do...

Whenever you are in the presence of a young child who is trapped in their own lie, remember that very young children cannot yet distinguish between the truth and lies. As their brain begins to integrate, they may be moved to lie in order to avoid getting into trouble or to preserve the connection they have with you, but even then, lying is an indication that brain development is happening. By not shaming, blaming, or punishing them for their dishonesty, you're providing a safe and accepting space for them to share the truth with you without fear of harsh repercussions. This will become part of the foundation that will be needed for parenting them through their teen years and beyond.

Today's parenting affirmation: I am encouraging my child to tell the truth by not overreacting to their lies.

33. My Whining Is Supposed to Aggravate You

. . . .

FOR MANY parents, the sound of a whining child is as irritating and tormenting as the noise of fingernails scraping along a chalkboard. Although whining grabs our attention and is almost impossible to ignore, it seldom elicits a caring response from those on the receiving end. If anything, it typically provokes a hostile reaction and it's known to move parents to do almost anything to try and shut it down as quickly as possible.

I've been in the presence of many whining children, and I've seen a wide range of parental reactions to it. Some react with visible irritation or blatantly ignore the child; others respond with the patience of a saint, and then there are those who resort to using sarcasm. One mother who had reached her limit and could no longer take the constant whining of her four-year-old son turned to him with a straight face and asked, "Would you like some cheese with that whine?"

At first, I didn't quite get what she was asking him. A few seconds later it made sense and although I enjoyed her adult wit and her well-meaning attempt to defuse her frustration, my heart went out to her little boy as I saw a mix of confusion and embarrassment wash across his face. His immature attempt to connect with her had garnered the opposite of what he was seeking, and she had unwittingly disconnected even further from him. Neither of them got what they were hoping for in this interaction.

Many parents are unaware that whining is in fact a step up on the developmental ladder. When a child develops the ability to whine, they're actually making progress. Consider it this way: babies don't yet have words and when they want attention, they're innately moved to cry. We may find this upsetting, or at times even stressful, but we know it's just their way of asking us to respond to them.

Toddlers take this babyish behaviour a step further by screaming and adding in simple verbal objections like the word "no," which may come out as a whiny and woeful "Noooooooooooo!" If we are provoked by their annoying communication, we don't respond to them as the immature little beings they are, and we may react by admonishing them for their inability to communicate more sensibly with us.

Young children, from around the age of three, add whining to their expanding repertoire of connection-seeking behaviours. Unless we know this, we assume they're being intentionally difficult by not using their big kid voices or "using their words." By whining they're trying to move from only making infantile sounds to also using words to express their wants and needs, but this is typically difficult to do when they're feeling tired, overwhelmed, frustrated, or unwell. With time, their spoken words will become more readily accessible, and they'll begin to communicate in a more mature way that will be considered more socially acceptable and far less grating on their parents' nerves.

While there's always a good reason behind whining, in our hurry to shut it down, we may inadvertently miss what that is. Sometimes children whine because they're tired, hungry, or not feeling well. Other times they don't want to accept the answer we have given as final and they're hoping to wear us down and change our minds. More often than not, the biggest reason that lurks beneath all those I've mentioned, is the child's deep need to release their pent-up frustration with a really good cry. By whining they're hoping to draw us into connection, so we'll be the ones to comfort them through their disappointment and sadness when their tears finally come. Seldom do we see their whining behaviour as an invitation for connection because it's so masked by their abrasive behaviour. As a result, we often back out of connection when we should be lovingly leaning in to provide it.

Parents who follow the outdated advice to just ignore a whining young child, may unwittingly exacerbate the underlying need fuelling the whine rather than meeting it. Similarly, the pervasive tendency to shame or scare a child into no longer whining might temporarily shut down this immature form of expression of frustration. But it will find another outlet, sometimes at a cost to their emotional development.

If we are to support young children to grow through their whining phase rather than getting stuck in it, we must give up the false belief that meeting their need with closeness and connection will reinforce their propensity to whine. A child who feels connected is not moved to act out in irritating ways in an effort to earn their parent's attention. If anything, a child who feels seen and heard has no need to work for attention because they can rest in knowing they already have it.

Here's what you can do...

When your young child grates on your nerves with an annoying whiny voice, pay attention to them. Instead of ignoring, mimicking, or telling them off for their irritating tone, simply draw them in closer by lifting them up or asking what you can do to help them. You will likely not get a direct answer because they might not have the words or even know what's troubling them. But your willingness to connect with them in their unsettled state will position you to connect with them when they need your presence most.

Today's parenting affirmation: I will give my whining child my loving attention because that's what they need most right now.

34. My Tantrums Are Gifts in Disguise

WHEN YOU first read that statement, you were likely quite taken aback and may have thought something along the lines of, "If that's the case, I'd like to return my gift immediately!" Seldom do parents consider the upside of tantrums.

As parents, we get to experience all of our young children's behaviours: the pleasant, the not-so-pleasant, and everything in between. Once we let them into our hearts, we're committing to love them just as they are and then it's up to us to figure out how to lovingly support them to grow in our presence. Within each tantrum awaits an opportunity for us to do just that. There's a gift for the child, one for the parents, and one for the relationship we share.

Tantrums are loud and upsetting because they're emotionally uncomfortable for the child, who is bumping up against the futility of what they can't have, can't do, or can't change. When they're engulfed by their upset, their irrational behaviour lets us know it. There may be kicking, screaming, biting, spitting, and hissing—all of which communicate the intensity of their struggle against a limit, lack, or loss. The realization of not being able to change what is, is very hard for them, but our being there to help them navigate their upset is what empowers them to be transformed by that which they cannot change.

When we know this, what's needed from us becomes clearer. We begin to focus less on addressing their abrasive behaviour head-on and instead put more focus on helping them to move from being fiercely mad to feeling deeply sad. With every tantrum comes the opportunity for parents to softly draw out their children's sadness and tears in the aftermath of their upset. Each time we do, we promote a little more resilience in the young child who, over time, comes to see that they can and do survive not having things their way. That's a gift.

It's emotionally rattling and frustrating to be a parent in the presence of a child having a tantrum, but understanding what's going on for them, and for us, makes all the difference. What appears to trigger the tantrum isn't where we ought to put our attention, it's how we hold space for the young child to move through their upset state that is most important. Not being sucked into trying to control the child in our blind panic will empower us to invite them to trust us with their big feelings. We always need to value their emotional expression ahead of our desire to teach them self-regulation and socially appropriate behaviour. There will be plenty of time for that as they grow. For now, they most need our understanding and our loving presence because these gifts will benefit them for a lifetime.

The emotions our children's tantrums stir up inside of us give us a glimpse into our own emotional maturity, but only if we're courageous enough to look. By being willing to reflect on our shortcomings, we open ourselves up to expanding our patience and tempering our reactions. By growing ourselves and loving them through it all, we convey to our children that we're there for them, we've got them, and nothing they do or say can ever diminish our love for them. There is no greater gift for a child and the relationship we share with them than that.

....

Here's what you can do...

When your child erupts in foul frustration, and they behave in ways that trigger you, remind yourself that wonderful gifts await both of you as you move through their tantrum. Looking at them as needing your help rather than your wrath in that very moment will boost the caring feelings you have for them and this will help you to manage your response to their over-the-top out-burst. Although this won't be easy to do at first, with practice and the willingness to support their healthy emotional development, you'll begin to find your way. Your deep love for them will make sure of that.

....

Today's parenting affirmation: I'm open to seeing my child's tantrums as opportunities for us both to grow.

35. Being Left Out or Ignored Really Hurts Me

· ·

IF IT hasn't already happened, it's only a matter of time before your young child comes to you to report they're feeling left out or ignored by a friend, sibling, or perhaps an adult. As their parent, you might experience a deep sense of sadness that one of life's hardest lessons has found them at such a young age, or perhaps it will evoke in you an intense feeling of annoyance that anyone would dare snub your precious child. Either way, your reaction is being driven by your own experiences of what it feels like to be ignored.

As parents it's heart-wrenching to know our children are feeling this way, and worse still, that they may be right about being left out. It's also a stark and humbling reminder that we can't control how other people make them feel. Although we try to choose their friends, orchestrate their play dates, supervise their activities, and keep a watchful eye on their interactions, none of this can guarantee their feelings won't get hurt. Not all is lost though.

Contrary to what many believe, not being able to protect children from feeling rejected doesn't leave them bereft nor us powerless. As long as we're not the ones doing the wounding, we can cultivate their resilience by establishing a secure relationship. When we consistently relate to them in caring and attentive ways, we provide them with an invisible shield, which protects their hearts as they navigate the inevitable hurtful interactions that come their way.

If being ignored by a friend or a sibling is emotionally wounding, imagine how much more hurt is felt when the person doing the ignoring is the parent they look to for their sense of belonging and significance. I'm not implying that occasionally being overlooked by the person you love is emotionally damaging. Nor am I knocking the well-placed advice that you limit the amount of attention you give typical childish habits like nose-picking and touching of genitals. I'm specifically referring to the wounding that occurs when a child is habitually ignored, given the silent treatment, or made to feel their presence is not valued or important.

Young children lack the brain development required to consider the multitude of reasons why others may exclude or ignore them. They don't comprehend that sometimes their behaviour is so off-putting that certain people withdraw their attention because those people can't tolerate the discomfort their behaviour evokes inside of themselves. Young children may assume that if they are consistently met with aloof or disinterested responses from others, they are solely to blame and there must be something wrong with them. They cannot consider the very real possibility that a parent who is emotionally distant may behave in detached ways because they are stressed, overwhelmed, or chronically depressed for their own reasons. As such, young children personalize rejection by others and blame themselves for the aloof treatment they receive even when it has nothing to do with them.

When a young child believes they are the reason they are not receiving their parent's loving attention, they will start to work to get it. They may intuitively adapt their behaviour to endear themselves to their parents. Once they discover they can earn the warm responsiveness they need to feel special and significant, they may alter themselves to get it. This comes at a cost to their long-term healthy emotional development because they grow up to believe that in order to maintain relationships, they have to earn another's loving attention and can't rest in knowing they are enough just as they are. Once young children stray into the unsatiating territory of feeling unworthy and unlovable, there's a risk that they'll become adults with low self-esteem who put pleasing others ahead of honouring and appreciating themselves.

Here's what you can do...

When you feel tempted to ignore your child, try and identify your motivation for feeling moved to do so. Your true reasons for withdrawing from them likely have little or nothing to do with them. Keep in mind that your child's need to be seen by you is so vital to their healthy emotional development that they'll do what they can to feel worthy of your loving attention, including adapting who they truly are in an effort to please you. By becoming aware of what's going on for you, you'll begin to change your ways of being with them, so they no longer have to.

If you are struggling with this aspect of parenting, consider seeking the support of a professional counsellor or therapist.

Today's parenting affirmation: I am willing to believe I am capable of being emotionally available for my child.

36. I Don't Want That Baby Anymore

ALTHOUGH WE expect it, nothing can fully prepare us for what it will feel like to have our child announce they don't like or don't want the new baby who has moved in. It took my eldest daughter a week or two to start objecting to the presence of her younger sister, and when she did, she made her feelings known. The novelty of the titles of "Big Sister" and "Mommy's Helper" had worn off and the reality of having to share everyone and everything she loved with the new arrival became too much for her. Her objections were compelling and her suggestions for getting rid of her little sister were creative and often amusing to adults.

Young children are self-centred and egotistical, and they're not very good at sharing. None of this is their fault; these are all attributes of their current state of immaturity. It's not that they're incapable of experiencing caring feelings toward the little sibling, it's that they can't care about their sibling's needs when they're not getting their own met as promptly or as attentively as they previously were. This is a huge obstacle for young children who have to adapt to the new order of things. As with all of us, change can be hard, but for a young child it is even more challenging.

How young children communicate their objection to the presence of their siblings will vary. Those who are capable of verbalizing their thoughts and feelings may communicate their sentiments using words, but given their current state of immaturity, will lack consideration for anyone's feelings other than their own. They might say tactless things like, "I want to give this baby away" or "I hate this baby." There may even be times when they intensify their objection and say something as malicious as "I'm going to kill this baby." This can really rattle parents who want to raise their children to love and care for each other.

Because young children can't easily identify the discomfort and frustration they're experiencing as feelings of displacement, they may not use words to communicate directly. Instead they often resort to what is commonly referred to as behavioural regression. What words can't tell us, behaviour can. Children who are feeling displaced may revert to using baby talk or may insist on being carried or cuddled as if they were still infants. Some may lapse in their toileting ability, alter their eating preferences, or even change up their sleep patterns. All this adds to the stress on parents who are trying to establish a new normal in their household.

As parents, we must be mindful about not getting pulled into admonishing the young child for their immature expression at the expense of addressing what's driving their behaviour. By acknowledging that they're feeling left out or pushed aside because of their younger sibling, we can pull them into deeper connection and allow them to feel heard and understood. Being made to feel special and told they are important to us is what they most need. Opportunities to help them find less hurtful words and less harmful ways to share their feelings will come with time and maturity. That's when they'll be better able to express themselves in more socially appropriate ways.

The key to finding the way through is knowing that regressive behaviour is natural and is the young child's way of communicating they're feeling insecure and aren't quite sure of where they fit in the newly expanded family puzzle. With time and some extra patience, you'll find your new flow and so will your children.

Here's what you can do...

Although it is heartbreaking to hear your child protest the presence of their new sibling, anticipating your young child's objection and seeing it as normal will empower you to respond in ways that support them to adapt to the arrival of a new baby. By reading their behaviour and inviting them to share their big feelings with you, you'll draw them into a deeper connection, and they'll once again feel seen, heard, and understood. Most important, they'll know they're special to you, even though the pesky baby is here to stay.

Today's parenting affirmation: I will find ways to make my older child feel seen, heard, and loved by me.

37. Let's Make It Fun

EVERY PARENT knows what it feels like to be pulled into a battle with an uncooperative child. Although we can sense ourselves being sucked in, we seem to go there anyway, and repeat the same behavioural patterns that haven't worked out many times before.

The biggest sinkholes in my early parenting days were when my children were cranky and I was feeling worn out. On some nights our dinnertime, bath time, and bedtime routines seemed to bring out the worst in us. The more resistant and challenging my daughters became, the more I would try and hurry them along by firmly insisting they do what I had asked so we could get the drill done and I could have a little well-deserved "me time" at the end of a long day.

When young children don't do what we want them to do, it's not unusual for parents to barge ahead and start explaining all the reasons why they need to co-operate. This is a surefire way to escalate the situation. Although young children are capable of understanding our words, if they don't feel like following our instructions, they won't. It's that simple. In these situations, parents are easily tempted to try and up the ante by justifying their stance and if that doesn't work, we start emphasizing the ramifications of what will happen if children fail to co-operate. In doing so, we make things much harder on ourselves and on them when we really don't have to. A little understanding of where young children are developmentally will support us to find a more pleasant way through.

A child who is resisting brushing their teeth or getting into the bathtub is doing so because in that very moment, they aren't feeling self-motivated to do it. Inconvenient but true. Understandably, this is very frustrating for logical adults with an agenda, but for the child it's simply a combination of not wanting to and not being developmentally capable of considering the implications of their refusal. Their reasons to resist aren't well thought out; their resistance merely indicates that they're focusing on something other than what we want them to do. Once we know this, it becomes more evident as to what we can do about it.

Knowing that young children are wired for play helps us to navigate their resistance before it morphs into a skirmish. A little game, a playful tickle, or a chance to giggle appeals to children and gets their attention. By infusing a bit of fun, we not only distract the non-integrated child from remembering they don't actually want to do something, but more important, it draws them back into connection with us and they're more likely to follow our lead. That's where our energy is best spent.

When we focus our attention on noticing where the struggles typically happen, we can get ahead by finding creative ways to change things up. If bath time has become a daily source of friction, we can try something like playing a chasing game in the direction of the bathroom to get them there. Or if washing is the issue, playfully using a water jet to rinse them off can help us to get the job done. Bedtime struggles can be softened by doing a puzzle or drawing a picture together before having the usual storytime. Having fun supports getting what needs doing done, and we all have a more enjoyable time doing it. Yes, it takes a little more time, effort, and enthusiasm, but if it leads to a more peaceful and pleasant interaction, isn't it worthwhile? Will it work every time? No, but it will work some of the time and this allows everyone to feel better.

Using fun to dissolve resistance can be helpful, but be wary of using it as a technique. Children are very perceptive and when we're using fake fun as a manipulative method of control, they sniff out our disingenuous attempt at engaging them for our own gain. Whenever we use fun to get us through the struggles, we'd better be authentic about it and make sure that we muster up genuine playfulness, or the results will speak for themselves.

Here's what you can do...

Avoid resorting to logical and lengthy explanations when trying to garner the co-operation of your young child. Your reasoning is lost on them, not because they don't understand your words, but because they don't feel like doing what you're insisting upon. By having more fun with them, you'll find enjoyable ways to get them to do what needs to be done. Being more playful is not only good for both of you, it will nurture your connection and serve your relationship well in the long term.

Today's parenting affirmation: I am open to being more playful, especially when we need to get things done.

38. It's Really Hard for Me Not to Interrupt You

HAVING A young child repeatedly interrupt when you're engaged in a conversation with someone is probably high on your list of frustrating parental experiences. When my daughters were younger, they seemed to have the most to tell me when my ears were the least accessible. Trying to make a phone call in their presence was almost impossible as it evoked a sense of urgency to get my attention. Needless to say, my patience diminished as their persistence increased and seldom did the interaction end peacefully.

Young children find waiting their turn difficult at the best of times. They may be slightly more receptive to being held off when you're doing something in their presence, but they're typically less tolerant of being stalled when you're engaged with another person. It becomes exponentially more challenging for them when they sense your attention is being given to another person because this intensifies their need to connect with you.

A young child's need for connection comes before their ability to remember their manners. This is particularly true when they feel they need to compete with another person to attract your attention back to them. During these moments they are naturally moved to try and close the perceived gap between you and them. Their need to connect is so powerful it overrides their ability to recall the many times you've already explained to them why interrupting you is not okay. Herein lies the source of much parental frustration because we're left wondering why when they seemingly know better, they don't do better!

Developmentally, their brains aren't yet wired to remember what they want to tell you at the same time as they hold on to the fact that you've repeatedly asked them not to interrupt you. Although they have logically understood the reasons why it's inappropriate to do so and they've likely promised you next time they won't interrupt (and they really mean it), they can't access these thoughts in the same moment they're thinking about what it is they need to tell or show you. Sharing your reasoning with them is never wasted, it's just not readily accessible to them in the moment because of their current immaturity.

As parents, we need to keep in mind that although we can't hurry nature and rush our children's development, we can adjust our expectations and contain our own reactions when we're being interrupted. Coming down harshly on a young child for interrupting doesn't address what's driving them to interrupt. If anything, it works against what they're trying to get right now—more connection.

It's not always practical or possible to give young children our undivided attention all the time. That's why we need to become resourceful rather than resentful. Making phone calls when they're not around is ideal. When it's not an option, distracting or redirecting them can be the way to go. It might be that giving them something to entertain them for a while is all that's needed. Perhaps inviting them onto your lap and making funny facial expressions while you talk on the phone might buy you the time you need to finish your conversation. There are multiple ways to work around being interrupted, but finding our way starts with our willingness to accept that interrupting is part of the young child's developmental journey. With time and maturity, they'll grow into not always having to be the focus of our attention, but for now, that's exactly what they need to be.

Here's what you can do...

Whenever you find yourself being interrupted by your young child, remind yourself they might not yet be developmentally capable of stopping themselves from doing so. Admonishing them for their rudeness might temporarily suspend their efforts, but it's not going to address their preeminent need for connection. As best you can, for now, try not to put them in situations where they'll be inclined to interrupt you. When that's not possible, do what you can to distract or engage them in pleasant ways in an attempt to buy yourself the time you need.

Today's parenting affirmation: I trust that as my child matures, they will be less prone to interrupting me.

39. Digital Devices Take Me Away from You

· ·

I AM frequently asked by parents for my opinion on giving young children digital devices. It often surprises them to hear that I don't object to children having them, but I am very concerned about what young children miss out on when they are using them.

Parents are the gateway between digital devices and children. That's a scary thought, but at the same time, it's an empowering realization. Ideally, we should think carefully about why we're putting devices into children's hands long before we introduce them to technology. Deciding how and when electronic devices will be used comes with great responsibility.

Unfortunately, many parents don't really think it through because it's difficult to consider the ramifications that haven't occurred to us yet. There are plenty of compelling reasons to give young children screen time, and some of them make sense. But doing so too early and too often can come at a cost to their development and to the quality of the heart connections they'll make with people around them.

I believe the often-used justification of "sooner is better" is misguided when it comes to introducing children to technology. Young children are unlikely to be better off in the future just because they were exposed to digital devices at an early age. Technology advances at such a rapid rate; what exists today will likely be obsolete long before they become teenagers. More than that, if adults can figure out how to use the latest gadgets, we're proof that we didn't need to learn how to use them as young children. When humans are motivated to learn how to do something, we do.

Unfortunately, just like television, handheld digital devices have the potential to become babysitters. I certainly took advantage of sometimes plopping my toddlers in front of the television to keep them in one place while I prepared a meal or used the bathroom in peace. Technology is meant to make our lives better and using it this way some of the time did exactly that. We shouldn't beat ourselves up for using technology to our advantage, but we should be mindful of how much we're relying on it as a substitute for our presence.

A tremendous amount of research and money goes into creating electronic educational games for young children. They most certainly absorb a lot of new information, develop cognitive skills, and have a lot of fun while playing these games. This exposure to academic material may result in elevated scores in certain areas when assessed by standardized tests, but we must never be misled into thinking devices are developing the whole child.

Young children learn best in the warmth and connection of our presence. Devices will never be a substitute for the optimal learning conditions created when a young child feels safe and secure in their relationships. We must be mindful of our tendency to subdue our parental guilt of leaving children to spend hours playing games by telling ourselves they are learning and therefore aren't missing out on engaging with others.

Looking around, I get the sense that young children today are not getting the same invitations to interact with those they love nearly as often as in generations gone by. It's not that we love them any less, it's that we've found a mobile and convenient way to entertain them when we have other things to do or just want a break. Parents need respite, but I worry about how much time we're missing out on connecting with young children because we've found a way to engage them, which draws them in so powerfully they don't seem to notice our absence.

Before digital devices existed, young children were more likely to sit in the discomfort of feeling bored long enough to generate their own ideas of things they could do to amuse themselves. Without the allure of an easy option to quell their boredom at the press of a button, young children sought out the company of their parents and siblings, or, if feeling moved to, they found ways to entertain themselves.

Many imaginative inventions, make-believe worlds, and creative works of art have emerged from children who had the opportunity to find their way out of having nothing to do. As long as young children feel content in the presence of attentive parents and are free of the temptation to turn on their devices, they'll be naturally moved to connect with others and to play, which is exactly what they need to be doing to promote their healthy emotional development.

Here's what you can do...

Each time you go to put a digital device into the hands of your young child, pause to consider your motivation for doing so. Be honest with yourself: is it in your child's best interest, or is it in your best interest to have them engage with a device rather than connect with you? Sometimes giving them screen time may be just what you both need, but at other times, you may be acting blindly out of habit. With practice, making the decision on how to proceed will become clearer because you'll begin aligning your decisions with your heartfelt intentions.

Today's parenting affirmation: I will reflect on my true motivations before handing my child a digital device.

40. Five-Minute Warnings Aren't Always Helpful

AS ADULTS we know from life experience that all good times eventually come to an end. Young children are only just beginning to learn this, and it's up to parents to break the news that it's time to stop what they're doing and leave when they are having fun. Given that we don't like upsetting children, it makes sense that we would want to ease them into accepting that the end is drawing near. Many parents give five-minute warnings to communicate how much time is left before the inevitable has to happen.

I once had the opportunity to sit and observe an interaction from start to finish of a mother giving her young children a countdown at the play park. They were having a great time digging in the sand, and they didn't seem nearly finished building the "cement factory" they were working on. It was obviously getting closer to the time their mother had planned to head home, and she gave a ten-minute heads-up followed by a minute-by-minute countdown from five to zero. With each minute ticking past I noticed the youngest boy appeared to be getting more agitated. Rather than getting increasingly mad as many children do, his panic seemed to flood him. He frantically tried to hurry what he was doing and the more flustered he became, the more dismally his efforts failed. By the time one minute was called his eyes were wide, his hands were shaking, and he began to get frustrated with things not working out for him. He hit the collapsed mound of sand with a shovel and let out a loud screech of infuriation. His mother was not impressed. She stormed over to him and admonished him for his inappropriate behaviour. Her harsh reaction to his outburst happened because she hadn't seen what had prompted it. She had no way of knowing that the countdown had stressed him out and frustrated him. She had intended to help him transition, but the opposite effect was achieved, and the interaction that followed resulted in discord between them.

Experience as a preschool teacher has shown me that countdowns are not helpful to all children. Some take them in their stride and others do not. For some, knowing the end is approaching is helpful; for others it's a highly alarming experience. For those who do not take a five-minute warning as it is meant, which is to be an opportunity to wrap up what they are doing, they panic and think, "I've *only* got five minutes left!" and this totally unnerves them. I've seen children become increasingly panic-stricken as the countdown gets closer to zero. It's as though they can't focus on what they need to be doing, because they are so thrown by the thought of not having enough time to finish. More often than we're aware, we inadvertently rattle children by not paying close attention to the effects our methods are having on them, and we make situations more stressful and intense for everyone involved.

Another aspect for parents to consider is our tendency to distort time when we use countdowns. If you've ever done a countdown, it's possible that you make the minutes as long or short as you want them to be. When we're having a good time chatting to our friends, we start the countdown, but then our minutes become very long minutes. Our five-minute warning might be more like fifteen minutes when counted on a clock. Keep in mind that although young children don't yet have much of a concept of real time, they most certainly don't understand our use of inconsistent time. One day they'll get an extra twenty minutes to play and the next our five minutes is closer to three because we're in a hurry to get going. That seems really unfair, especially if we get frustrated with them for not adhering to our time frame.

Our focus needs to be on what effect our countdowns are having on children. If they are becoming increasingly agitated or resistant, it's an indication they are struggling with accessing their feelings of sadness and disappointment around not being able to continue what they are doing. Once we're aware of this, we're able to see them as needing our help to adapt to what they can't change, and we tailor our approach to direct them in other ways. While we should always anticipate some pushback, at least we won't blindly continue to use an approach that consistently derails them.

Here's what you can do...

Pay closer attention to your child's response to five-minute warnings and countdowns. Do they find it exciting and motivating? Or do they experience it as overwhelming or distressing? If you have a child who responds well to it, try and be more consistent by using a clock so they begin to develop a sense of time. If your child is alarmed by countdowns, give it a break for a while and perhaps try again when they are a little older. By being mindful of the effect of a countdown, we can make simple adjustments to our ways and avoid turning transitions into times of unnecessary conflict.

Today's parenting affirmation: I will notice how my child responds to countdowns and I can change my methods if necessary.

41. Stories Help Me Connect with You

WHEN MY children were babies, they didn't mind what I read to them. As long as my lips were moving and I looked their way, they were content to listen to me read anything I had in front of me. It didn't matter if it was a magazine, a travel brochure, or the obituaries. For them, it was all about me being physically close to them and feeling connected to me because of the sounds and facial expressions I made in their direction. Anyone listening in might have thought I had gone off the deep end, but I knew exactly what we were doing. We were connecting.

As they grew, I introduced board books with pictures and the odd printed words. I'd point to the pages, gesture with my hands and ask rhetorical questions. Their eyes would get wide, they'd make sounds to approximate words and I'd respond as if they were making the most thoughtful contributions to our discussions. Interacting in this way became something we looked forward to doing and before long, they started requesting that we read together, sometimes many times a day!

When young children are invited to listen to a story or read a book with their loved ones, their developing brains become sponges eager to absorb what is shared. They don't need to be formally taught how to speak, they simply need to be spoken to and they'll pick up words along the way. Not only do young children expand their vocabulary, they also figure out how to sequence words and use intonation in preparation for communicating effectively with others.

Parents often worry about young children who resist speaking. They may understand what is being said, but they continue to rely on making infantile sounds and gestures to communicate their wants or needs. In these situations, I encourage parents to remain patient and to resist resorting to drawing their child's attention to their inability or seeming unwillingness to speak. Some children simply need more time before they feel ready to speak. I have known many children labelled as "strong and silent types" who resist saying single words, but one day blurt out coherent sentences.

It is often said that readers are created in the laps of their parents. While I have found this to be true of my own children, not all young children like to sit down and read, yet they still learn to read. As parents, we must be mindful of not clinging so tightly to our intention to grow children into readers that we sabotage our connection along the way. Trying to forcefully get a child to attend to something that doesn't interest them, or requires more attention or co-operation than they're currently able to give, must not result in a battle. Introducing board books at mealtimes or using special waterproof bath books at bath time may be a way of engaging young children with books in situations when they're not required to focus exclusively on being read to. That said, sometimes the very best thing we can do is back off and remember that we can always try reading to them in the future.

Bedtime stories are one of the highlights of many young children's bedtime routines. It's a time of closeness and connection with loved ones, which is exactly what children need before they close their eyes and drift off to sleep. After a long day, parents may forget this and fall into the trap of wanting to rush through a book to get to the concluding words: "The End." Nothing draws out the request for more stories quite like a child who senses your urgency to get out the door. Be mindful of the energy you bring with you to bedtime stories, as not showing up with warmth and genuine enjoyment will likely have the opposite effect you're hoping for.

Not all parents are able to read to their children. There are many adults who were not able to learn to read themselves. This does not have to hinder their ability to connect with their children through sharing stories. A parent holding a book and making up words is just as enjoyable for a young child as hearing the original words of the author. Even just telling a child a story without a book is enough to draw them in and delight them. The point is to connect with them, not to impress them, and so, with a little imagination and a willing heart, parents can do exactly that.

Some parents do not live with their children, but manage to get creative about still reading to them. I know parents who read stories over the phone or on a video call and some who send voice recordings so their children get to know their voice even though they may not be together for extended periods of time. Using books in this way has the capacity to open up channels of connection across great distances and keep children feeling close to their parents even when they are miles apart.

Here's what you can do...

By inviting your young child to sit with you and read a book, or listen to you tell them a story, you're connecting with their heart and expanding their mind. They do not need to be formally taught words in order to learn how to communicate, they simply need to feel connected to you in order to remain open to learning what you have to share with them. As they grow and develop, their interest in learning to read for themselves will be nurtured because of the stories you have enjoyed together.

If you are concerned about your child's language development, consider consulting a speech-language pathologist.

Today's parenting affirmation: I can use books and stories to draw my child into deeper connection with me.

42. Not Getting My Own Way Can Be Good for Me

WHEN MY children were young, there were many times where I would deliberately manipulate conditions in order to buy myself a little peace. I was tired of dealing with the drama that would unfold over the smallest of things, and I figured that by making things right, fair, or easier for my daughters, the day would be more pleasant for us all.

At first, making sure the sandwiches were equal-size triangles and that the juice was in matching cups with exactly the same amount in each seemed like a small inconvenience for a peaceful payoff. It worked most of the time, but I found myself running in circles trying to anticipate the potential land mines, and then doing whatever I could to try and keep them from detonating. I began to realize that being a "fixer" was exhausting. It became clear that I could never keep up with ensuring everything was perfectly fair or just how they wanted it, and I couldn't always save my children from their upset.

While it may be tempting to take the easy route and to buy peace by doing whatever we can to spare the child from their emotional discomfort, each time we do so we're unwittingly doing them a disservice. Our well-intentioned efforts may seem like the path of least resistance in the moment, but our actions can have long-term ramifications. They need to learn eventually that everything may not always go exactly the way they want.

When we hastily try and prevent or fix a problem in order to keep the peace, we're also attempting to alleviate our own irritation and discomfort as quickly as possible.

Our role as a parent is not to try and change the world to suit the child, but rather to gently help the child adapt to their world. As adults, we've had many years to learn that not everything goes the way we want, and some of us are still coming to terms with this. Young children are only just beginning to discover how things work. Much of their day is filled with frustration and upset because they encounter devastating realizations like not always being able to have what they want, not being able to have more of what is finished, not always being the best, not being able to fix what's broken, and not being able to make good experiences last forever. The list of futilities they face seems endless and they begin to see that life can be hard sometimes. They rightfully have a lot to be upset about, and we need to be mindful of this.

When young children are confronted by a limitation, restriction, or unmovable boundary and we allow our hearts to go out to them during their struggle, our reactions naturally transform into softer responses. By not being too hasty to fix circumstances or placate them in an attempt to redirect or control their emotion, we support the developmental process of adaption, which is pivotal to building resilience. Seeing them as immature little beings who are having a hard time coming to terms with how the world works makes us less hasty to try and fix circumstances or appease young children in an attempt to suppress or control their emotions.

It's in our willingness to allow our children to experience their big emotions that some of our greatest opportunities to support their emotional development await. When children are able to feel their upset in the presence of someone who will lovingly be there for them, they begin to realize they can and do survive when they don't get their own way. Resilience isn't taught with hard lessons; it's grown during interactions with those who care enough to be with us during our times of emotional discomfort, so we're not tempted to try and block it out. When young children move through their emotional discomfort with someone they love by their side, they are changed for the better by the experience.

Always keep in mind that there will be times when it's appropriate for us to make changes to accommodate the child. Not every situation is a viable opportunity to build the child's resilience. When they're not feeling well or have had a particularly unsettled or upsetting day, they would benefit most from being given a break from some things not going their way. Even as mature adults we still have those days, and we must recognize and meet the same needs in our children.

Here's what you can do...

When your child is struggling with frustration, upset, or disappointment, remember that it's natural for them to feel this way when faced with something that is not working for them. These emotional responses are an important and necessary part of identifying their feelings and coming to know themselves. While it may be tempting for you to consistently try and change the circumstances in an effort to spare their emotional upset or hurt feelings, every time you do, you rob them of an opportunity to grow another layer of resilience that will serve them well in years to come.

Today's parenting affirmation: I realize that trying to make everything work for my child will not help them build resilience.

43. Don't Try and Rush Me Toward Independence

OUR DAYS as parents are filled with opportunities to teach children how to do things for themselves. It's easy to forget that although young children are capable, they have a deep need to feel taken care of, and they depend on us. When we lose sight of this basic need, many ordinary interactions inadvertently become battlegrounds. We find ourselves insisting that they walk rather than be carried, that they tidy up their toys without our help, or they carry their own backpacks because they're big and strong. The impasse that follows is seldom resolved quickly or quietly and what starts out as a lesson in independence unravels into a scene of resistance and defiance.

While most parents readily agree that independence is high on the list of vital qualities to instill in growing children, how to go about teaching independence can be a contentious topic. We each bring our personal opinions, attitudes, and experiences to the conversation, and this makes navigating the terrain all the more confusing, particularly in a society that regards and reveres independence as highly as ours does. With this being the case, parents who are overtly promoting independence may be seen to be more sensible than those who appear to be coddling their children by being less demanding and more willing to help.

As the parent of two small children, I saw first-hand the perils of trying to push them toward independence.

I could see that when they weren't receptive to doing things for themselves, asserting my will didn't transmit the life skills and lessons I hoped it would. If anything, it evoked their resistance, my frustration, and our disconnection. I realized what was getting in the way was not their inability to behave independently, but their current state of unwillingness. In these situations, I could become coercive and employ tactics to make them brush their teeth, dress themselves, and put on their own shoes, but this turned ordinary daily activities into unpleasant altercations that resulted in their emotional detachment and unnecessary upset for us all.

Just because young children are capable of doing things for themselves some of the time, doesn't mean they should be expected to do it all of the time. Don't get me wrong, I'm not suggesting we do everything for young children all of the time. I'm simply recommending that parents consider the context of the situation before drawing a line in the sand as to what they will and won't do for children. Sometimes holding your ground does indeed promote their independence, but other times it will hinder it. Which way it goes depends on the present moment circumstances and the quality of the connection you share right then. Paying attention and trying to understand what's going on for your child is far more beneficial than blindly and relentlessly insisting they act independently.

The common misperception that children need to be taught to be independent is what frequently leads parents to trying to force it upon children. When young children can rest in knowing we have their backs and are there to help them, they're naturally moved to become curious and independent. They're also more willing to reach out and ask for help and to accept help when it is forthcoming. Their self-motivation and enthusiasm are completely different to the energy of a child who has been required to act independently out of necessity or fear of unpleasant repercussions. If one of our deepest desires as parents is to love and nurture children into becoming viable, independent adults, we can start by being there for them when they're young and need us most.

Here's what you can do...

If ever you find yourself in a deadlock with your young child because they refuse to do something independently, back up and consider offering them your help. Prematurely forcing independence on a young child may result in some independent behaviour, but it isn't likely to grow them up into adults who are able to ask for and accept help when they truly need it. In order for children to be willing to trust in people as they grow up, we need to consistently be there to help them when they're young and need our help the most.

Today's parenting affirmation: I am willing to offer my child help whenever I read them as needing it.

44. Please Don't Disappear on Me

A SUGGESTION sometimes made by well-meaning care-givers and teachers is that parents sneak off once their young child is occupied. Admittedly, this may seem like an attractive option, particularly if you want to avoid going through the upsetting experience of leaving a distressed child or you're under pressure to be somewhere else by a certain time. It makes sense from the perspective of a hurried adult, but when we consider the experience from the child's viewpoint, our take on the situation begins to shift.

As a preschool teacher, I've seen the devastated look on many children's little faces when they look up from what they are doing only to discover that their loved one has disappeared. Their expression goes from looking around expectantly, hoping to catch their parent's attention, to scanning the room in distress, to a look of sheer terror as they realize they have been left behind. It's as though time slows down for them as they try and make sense of the enormity of what has just happened. Some children move straight to tears of sadness, but others hold back their tears and block out their emotional discomfort. In the short term, suppressing their sadness may help them to function and appear to be fine, but if this happens repeatedly, over time they may unconsciously start avoiding their vulnerable feelings. The repercussions of doing so might initially not appear obvious, but as time passes, evidence of their emotional defences may surface in the form of other troubling behaviours.

Parents need to know there is nothing developmentally amiss with a child who shows distress when having to separate. They are being true to their instincts, and it is natural for them to want to stay close to whom they feel most attached. That said, because it isn't always practical or possible to be with our children all of the time, we need to find ways to help them to feel close to us even when we are physically apart. Simple things like drawing a heart on the palm of their hand to remind them they are loved or tucking a picture of a parent into their pocket might be just what they need to feel connected to their loved ones when they are not together.

Many parents worry that young children will never outgrow this stage, and they put their focus on reasoning with the young child trying to convince them to feel differently than they do. Once we understand that young children speak the language of connection rather than logic, we're able to subtly change our approach. Rather than drawing their attention to why we need to leave them, we can instead talk about when we'll be together again. This small shift in our approach conveys to the child that we will be united again. It lets them know that our love for them continues even when we are physically apart. Although this is not a quick fix for the tears and sadness that often ensue in the moment of departure, it does over time sink in for children as experience shows them we can be trusted to come back to them.

Here's what you can do...

As best you can, keep in mind that it's natural to feel upset when you have to leave your young child. It is understandably unsettling for them and for you. Every separation is an opportunity to convey that your love for them continues even when you're apart and they can trust others to take care of them when you're not around. Do what you can to strengthen the connection they have with their caregivers as once they are deeply attached to them, your leaving will be less alarming and upsetting for everyone.

Today's parenting affirmation: I need to always say goodbye so that my child will trust me to return.

45. I'm Not Out to Get You

BEFORE WELCOMING my own children, I formally studied education and human development for over a decade. During that time, I also taught and cared for other people's children. While I certainly learned much from my interactions with them, it wasn't nearly enough to prepare me for the magnitude of the emotional investment and the levels of frustration that being a parent of my own young children would someday bring.

When my daughters were younger, I sometimes wondered if they were deliberately out to get me. While we certainly had plenty of easygoing days, there were times when they would become what felt to me to be downright obstinate and challenging. It seemed as though they were intentionally pushing the boundaries and purposefully behaving in ways that fell outside the parameters of my expectations. Their lack of consideration for my feelings and appreciation for my efforts felt like a personal slight sometimes.

There were many nights I'd lie in my bed and question the value of my hard-earned education and the efficacy of my parenting efforts because despite my best attempts, my children still behaved in ways that were not to my liking. Sharing this now, I feel ashamed for how poorly I misinterpreted their inherently immature behaviour. Developmentally they weren't yet capable of behaving any better than they were, but back then, I couldn't help but feel as though their actions were intentional.

Having been there myself, I understand why many parents fall into the cycle of trying to change children's unwanted behaviour. When parents believe young children's behaviour is deliberate, it's easy to be tempted to resort to using a tit-for-tat approach to try and get them to improve their behaviour. The trouble with this method is that parents don't take the lead to guide their children through common struggles, and instead they join them in it. In these situations, because the parent's frustration escalates, the child's needs are often left unmet. Both parties are invariably left feeling hurt, controlled, smothered, or guilty for their words or actions.

If parents can appreciate and accept that young children are entitled to behave like immature little creatures, we're no longer as quick to assume they're intentionally trying to provoke us. Our deep love and desire to understand them better leads us away from blaming them for our discomfort. Instead we start looking inwardly at ourselves. Once we do, it becomes clear that they aren't out to get us; they just need us to "get" them. This shift in perception is exactly what we need to see our young children as the innocent beings they are. If we do, it can make our parent-child connection even stronger.

Here's what you can do...

If you find yourself feeling like your child is intentionally trying to make your life more difficult, remind yourself their actions are not premeditated, and they're not out to get you. They are developmentally immature beings who are living their lives the only way they currently know how, which is inconsiderately, but not vindictively. By keeping your focus on how you respond, you'll start to figure out how best to guide and direct them without sabotaging the connection you're longing to have with them. You'll also begin to understand yourself better than you ever have before.

Today's parenting affirmation: I am capable of responding to my child's immature behaviour with grace and understanding.

46. I Need Kindness Most When I Appear to Deserve It Least

SOME OF the most challenging encounters parents will ever endure occur in the presence of young children. Their immature reactions to not getting their way can be so over the top we find ourselves gritting our teeth, tensing our muscles, and muttering under our breath to contain ourselves from erupting into adult-sized tantrums. It seldom occurs to us during these infuriating circumstances that showing young children our understanding and compassion is even an option.

If you believe children should be admonished for their inappropriate behaviour, the notion of being kind to them when they're being challenging may sound ridiculous. You may wonder why anyone would indulge them with kindness when what they clearly need to learn is that their behaviour is unacceptable. From this place, being kind may not only seem counterintuitive, it might go against what you believe children need to experience in order to learn. This misinformation needs to be challenged.

If young children are expected to behave in particular ways to be deserving of our compassion, they are doomed from the start. They can't help but express their frustration in volatile, often offensive ways because they are immature beings who lack the ability to control their emotions. A young child who is engulfed by a tantrum can't behave any better than they currently are. Parents who don't yet know this will deem this type of behaviour to be outside the parameters of what deserves their benevolence and are likely to withhold from the child what they need most: kindness and compassion.

Some of the most valuable teaching opportunities and prospects for fostering connection with young children open up during their most horrid frenzies. If we can muster the awareness to see children as having a really hard time with their big emotions, we're led to softening our hearts and responding to them with compassion—particularly when their behaviour is at its worst. This does not mean we give up boundaries or let them have their way, it means we hold the boundaries firmly but gently and do not resort to withdrawing our kindness in an effort to get them to change their ways.

A young child who misbehaves requires gentle guidance and not harshness. When we're able to contain our reactions, we're more likely to redirect them in ways that do not shut them down emotionally and prevent them from taking in the lessons we want them to learn. True learning requires the child to be receptive to the adults trying to teach them and for that to happen, they must feel safe and taken care of within the relationship.

Here's what you can do...

When your young child is being flooded by their emotions, remind yourself that in this moment they can't behave any better than they currently are. Seeing them as an immature, vulnerable little being who needs your compassion will move you to show them kindness when their behaviour appears to warrant it least. A mantra that may help in your most trying moments could be: "When I don't know what else to do, I'll be kind."

Today's parenting affirmation: I choose to see my child as *always* being deserving of my kindness.

47. I Don't Make You Lose Your Temper, *You* Lose Your Temper

CONTRARY TO what many parents think, the arrival of children isn't what turns us into impatient people. All they do is bring our awareness to our current capacity to process frustration. Before they were part of our lives, we may not have seemed as short-tempered as we are now, but that's only because we were able to avoid many situations that were likely to result in a buildup of frustration. We could plan our day and execute it, arrange a time and stick to it, and, if we needed to, we could dodge some of the people who were likely to push our buttons. Our pre-children days probably included more downtime, sleep time, and "me time," which all naturally alleviated some of our stress. You get the picture; we had more say in how things were done, and so we intentionally evaded frustration in order to not experience it.

All that changes once children enter our lives. Their presence brings much anticipated joy along with exponential frustration that is more intense than we could ever have imagined. We have no choice but to face it head-on. Every resistance instead of co-operation, every slowing down instead of speeding up, every "no" when we want to hear a "yes," all add up and take us to the brink, or beyond.

When we add to our parenting frustration the common daily irritations like getting stuck in traffic, the internet going down, being unable to find a parking spot, or having a looming deadline at work, our emotional system feels like it's overloaded, and we can't help but release it. Unfortunately, unless we recognize what's happening for us, we may take it out on our children. We perceive them to be the cause of our frustration, when really they are the portal to us becoming more patient people.

What's going on is completely understandable, but discharging pent-up frustration onto anyone, especially vulnerable children, is unacceptable. When we repeatedly blame a child for our immature behaviour, we wound them emotionally. They grow up believing they are accountable for keeping those in power happy, and live in fear of the potential repercussions if they don't. There is no emotional rest in that space for them or for us, and it results in further frustration in the relationship we share.

To become self-aware is the way to change our behaviour for the better. Every frustrating interaction with our children is an invitation to look at what is really going on inside of ourselves. By paying attention to why we yell loudly at a child for leaving their backpack in the hallway or why we slam our hands down on the table when they don't eat their dinner, we begin to see this isn't only about their childish actions. Our reactive behaviour is being fuelled by the buildup of frustration in our emotional system and the hostile discharge is directed at them. It is up to each of us to acknowledge our part in the dynamic because only when we do, will we begin to take responsibility for our actions and change our disparaging behaviour.

Here's what you can do...

When you find yourself feeling frustrated by the words or actions of your child, be aware of your reaction. While your child's behaviour might be the source of some of your frustration, your child is ultimately not responsible for how you process your emotions. Each time you discharge your emotions at your children you give them the misguided message that they are responsible for your actions. That's not true. You are.

If you are struggling to control your temper, consider seeking the support of a professional counsellor or therapist.

Today's parenting affirmation: I am responsible for managing my own frustration.

48. You Should Apologize to Me

THERE WILL always be moments when our parenting actions do not align with our heartfelt intentions. Being human means our impatience sometimes gets the better of us, and we find ourselves doing and saying things to our children that we wish we hadn't. Tempers flare and feelings are hurt because we're moved by a powerful root emotion called frustration. Although parental acting out isn't ideal, it's understandable given all that happens in a day. Whenever we cross the line, we have an opportunity and a responsibility to own our actions and repair any fall-out we've left in our wake.

One question I frequently get asked by parents who've reacted in a fiery manner is, "Should I apologize to my child?" I believe the answer is always absolutely *yes*, especially if you're wanting to preserve the connection you have with them. Any time we withhold an apology for our out-of-bounds behaviour, we're not erasing it from their experience, we're intentionally denying that our actions had an effect on them. We convey the underlying message that our short-tempered behaviour doesn't matter, and their feelings aren't important. By not acknowledging our wrongdoings, we're undermining the very values we hope to teach them.

An apology to a young child should be short and sincere. The words we use aren't nearly as important as the energy that accompanies them. Communicating in a heartfelt way opens young children up to trust the genuineness of our apology. They don't want to hear lengthy explanations justifying what led to our outburst, and in that moment, they most certainly don't need to be told what they did to trigger our eruption of foul frustration. If need be, that can be revisited at another time.

Apologies aren't meant for teaching lessons as this detracts from their essence. They're intended to convey our vulnerability and willingness to own our actions. They also serve to repair any damage we may have done by restoring the connection we severed by behaving immaturely. By apologizing, we're not showing weakness or losing face, we're owning our mistakes and reaffirming our intention to do better in the future. There are many valuable and often unexpected benefits to be gained by freely giving a heartfelt apology, and we should never hold them back out of fear of what our children might think of us.

Here's what you can do...

When you blow it—and you will—don't be afraid to acknowledge your humanity and your mistakes. By owning your actions and giving a short and sincere apology, you'll be modelling the considerate behaviour you want your child to show toward others someday. Also, be sure to give yourself a little grace, not in an attempt to excuse yourself, but to keep your heart soft so that you can keep showing up for your children and become more like the parent you yearn to be.

Today's parenting affirmation: I will readily give my child a heartfelt apology when I make a mistake.

49. I Need to Feel Taken Care of by You

THE FIRST time I was asked if I thought my young children felt taken care of by me, I was baffled. I didn't quite know how to answer the question and so I began listing all the ways in which I took care of them. It had never occurred to me that how I took care of them might not be received by them as the loving care I intended it to be. After some conversation and reflection, it became clearer to me: taking care of a child and having that care sink in so they feel emotionally at rest in our care are two different things.

After that realization, I began to pay closer attention to the underlying messages my energy might be conveying to my children. Although I didn't for a second doubt my ability to take good care of them physically, I hadn't considered that my unconscious ways could inadvertently be hindering their emotional development. Nothing seemed obviously awry, but that conversation had me wondering if my well-meaning ways were unintentionally affecting their developing sense of security and well-being. I think this worry lurks in the back of every caring parent's mind and I decided to delve a little deeper into it.

It's been said that once you see something, you can't unsee it. This became very evident to me when I began to observe my parenting ways more closely. It became clear that some of my ways were deterring my young children from trusting in my ability to fully meet their needs. Although I was caring and attentive, I was sometimes undermining their trust in me by not considering how my actions may have felt to them from their perspective. The energy behind some of my actions was broadcasting my parenting insecurities and my sensitive child was particularly attuned to receiving the news.

I began to notice how often I asked them questions about their needs when it came to matters of caregiving. I was consulting them on simple things I should have trusted myself to know the right answer to. Questions like "Do you need a hug?" weren't necessary because I knew them so well and I could read them to get the answer. Yet I still asked. Not to suggest that asking young children for their preferences is bad, it's more a matter of what we're conveying to them when we constantly ask them questions about things for which we should already have the answers.

For example, if your partner knows you well, they should have a good idea of what to get you for your birthday. When they constantly ask you what they should buy you, they likely mean well, but the subtext to their question may make you feel as though they don't know you as well as you hoped they did. If this seemingly harmless inquiry makes you question the depth of an adult relationship, imagine what being asked too many questions does to an immature child who needs to feel known by their parents if they are to feel secure and taken care of by them.

Consistently asking questions in an attempt to please the child and avoid upsetting them is a common theme in many households. Asking for their opinions is not the issue, it's taking a look at *why* we're asking so many questions that needs to be inspected more closely. If it's because we live in fear of the wrath of a child who reacts explosively when we don't get something right, asking questions may be our timid way of trying to avoid the upset.

On a surface level, it makes sense that fact-finding before acting can buy peace some of the time; however, as young children grow up, this approach can make them feel insecure rather than taken care of. With time, some children start telling parents how to take care of them without even waiting to be asked the questions. Once this pattern gets established, parents find themselves walking on eggshells trying to predict and satisfy their children's demands rather than meeting their deepest need, which is to find emotional rest in their care.

In order for young children to feel taken care of, parents must provide them with a sense of being known. Children must be able to trust that we know them well enough to meet their needs because we read them, not because they tell us what to do for them. Any time we find ourselves resorting to asking questions around what they need so they won't get frustrated with us, we must catch ourselves and be aware that the unsure energy we're conveying is likely to undermine our caregiving rather than encourage it to sink in.

Here's what you can do...

When you find yourself frequently asking questions in order to avoid upsetting your young child, check in with your motives for doing so. While there is no harm in wanting to please your child, by consistently asking them what they need from you or how they want you to take care of them, you're unwittingly undermining their ability to completely trust in you to meet their needs. If your child is to rest in your care, they need to feel truly known by you.

Today's parenting affirmation: I am willing to believe I can trust myself to meet my child's needs.

50. You Don't Need to Hurt Me in Order to Teach Me

GETTING TO know children and their families is one of the greatest privileges of being a preschool teacher. I've always felt honoured to be in a profession that entrusts me with the responsibility of interacting with young children as they learn and grow. Often, what starts as brief daily greetings between parent and teacher evolve into deeper conversations about the well-being and development of children. Given that we're both invested in providing the most favourable conditions for children to thrive, it's no surprise when the topic of discipline arises.

One conversation that stands out took place with a dad just a few weeks after I started looking after his son. We were discussing how the boy had settled at preschool, and he asked about his willingness to follow my instructions. I said that he was a delightful little guy, eager to participate and keen to co-operate with me. The dad looked quite taken aback and then advised that it was only a matter of time before I saw his son's true colours. He proceeded to give me his express permission to "put him back into line" when he was no longer being obedient, and he gestured with his hands to demonstrate how I could go about doing that.

How we discipline children has to do with our personal experiences and beliefs as to what is necessary and effective. We're heavily influenced by our families and culture, and both create parameters around what we consider to be normal, acceptable parenting practices. That said, the excuses of previous generations for using physical punishment to discipline children no longer stand. There's a great deal of research-based evidence outlining the harmful effects of physical coercion and its detrimental effects on the healthy emotional development of young children. The internet instantly connects us to this information. At the click of a button, resources and people to support parents wanting to find alternatives to physical coercion are accessible to anyone.

The conversation I had with that dad all those years ago drew us closer together, not further apart. In a convoluted way, his suggestion that I use physical means to spur his son into obedience was his way of inviting me into the circle of adults he trusted to help raise his son. The method he was advocating was one his parents and grandparents had relied upon and he truly believed this was in the best interests of his young son. He wanted nothing more than to raise his son to someday become a caring and responsible adult, and this became the premise on which our future conversations revolved.

It wasn't my place to judge his beliefs, nor to point out what I considered to be flaws in his approach. My intention was to help him nurture the connection he was building with his son so that he could pass on his values and expectations in a way that would cultivate the long-term relationship he wanted to have with his little boy. His willingness and deep love for his son is what opened his heart and mind to not only consider a different approach, but also to find the courage to implement it.

Here's what you can do...

Having the courage to question your beliefs and the willingness to seek alternatives will support you to align your actions with your heartfelt intentions. If you have even a tiny inkling that physically hurting your child to correct their behaviour is wrong, pay very close attention to that. Your intuition is speaking to you and wants to guide you in the direction of finding gentle but effective ways to discipline the child you love.

Today's parenting affirmation: I am open to using a gentle approach to teach my child right from wrong.

51. Your Phone Takes You Away from Me

WHEN WE'RE looking at our phones, we don't even notice what we're missing out on. I was struck by this at a local park one day. I noticed two girls around the age of four interacting and having a fine time playing with a stick. Watching them engage with one another was delightful. One of the girls must have been saying something very intriguing because the other little girl was hanging on her every word. They shared a few giggles and then the chattier of the two looked over to her mom who was sitting on a bench a little distance away. She called to her to include her in the conversation, but I could see the mom was fully immersed in her phone. She didn't respond so the little girl tried again. Nothing. A look of disappointment and then sadness washed over the girl's face. She called out a final time and then scowled in annoyance before bolting across the playground toward her mother and intentionally bumping into her. That certainly got her mom's attention, but it also got the little girl into trouble for knocking into her and not using her words.

When we don't pay attention, we miss out. This mom had no idea that her daughter had tried to connect with her and include her in whatever was so entertaining about that stick. Not only did the mother miss out on an invitation for connection, she didn't see the delight on her daughter's face, and she ended the interaction with a scolding. Countless opportunities like this slip by unnoticed not because we're purposely ignoring our children, but because we're so drawn to our phones. It's impossible to feel sad about what we're unaware of missing out on, but recognizing that we don't want to miss out can inspire us to become more conscious of our ways.

Parents sometimes think that being physically present with a young child is enough. While children most certainly rely on our physical presence to feel secure, they're also counting on us to be attentive and to respond to them. When we get sucked into the internet vortex, we leave our bodies behind on the bench and our attachment energy gets funnelled away from those around us. Our young children experience our lack of engagement as disconnection, and that fuels attachment frustration. Many of the behavioural battles we endure on a daily basis would disappear if we were to notice and rectify how often we're checking out instead of checking in.

That said, it's no wonder we're so captivated by our phones, they're devices of attachment, and humans are creatures of attachment! Emails and texts connect us with others, but they can also disconnect us from those physically around us. Similarly, social media offers a glimpse into the life of someone else and this makes us feel somewhat connected to them. It's a superficial connection because we don't necessarily interact with them on a personal level, but our attachment-seeking brain doesn't really distinguish the difference. As long as we get a hit of what feels like connection, we're driven to seek more, and it can be very difficult to stop. Recognizing that social media is not a substitute for deep connection is the start of us changing our ways. By turning more of our attention toward our young children when they're in our company, we're naturally positioned to give and get what we're both longing for: more meaningful and personal connection.

As with all things in moderation, phones aren't bad. For many parents they are a welcome source of enjoyment, entertainment, useful information, and more often than we'd like to admit; the perfect distraction from what's going on emotionally inside of ourselves. We're fortunate to be parenting in an era where we can keep up with friends we don't have time to see, and can stay in touch with those who live far away. We can even join online communities that inspire and support us to become the parents we want to be. As long as we become more mindful of when and why we're staring at the screen, we'll limit their use and make sure we don't allow their existence to erode the relationships we value, especially the relationships we're newly cultivating with our young children.

Here's what you can do...

The next time you reach for your phone, look around at who is in your presence and consider how many opportunities for connection you could potentially miss out on if you're mindlessly engaged with your device. Your young child needs both your physical presence and your loving attention if they are to remain feeling connected to you as they grow.

Today's parenting affirmation: I am open to noticing how often I check out when I could be checking in.

52. I Can't Yet Fully Appreciate You

PARENTING CAN feel like a thankless job. There have been times when I have looked at my own children and thought, "A little gratitude would go a long way right about now." This didn't do anything to draw out their thanks and it further fuelled my discontent and feelings of being unappreciated. I know feeling this way is not helpful; but honestly, sometimes it seems unavoidable as my head just goes there. After a while, my woeful feelings of being underappreciated subside, my perspective returns and I'm better able to consider that perhaps my children aren't ungrateful out of malice, they're simply immature and unaware of just how much I do for them because they don't know any different.

While it's understandable that parents long to hear words of appreciation from their offspring, this isn't something children consciously make a point of doing. Young children are known to spontaneously gush a big "thank you," or a heartfelt "I love you" when we least expect it, but they don't do so because it's the right thing to do; they do it because that's how they feel in that particular moment. These unexpected gestures of pure appreciation burst out of them and they surprise themselves just as much as they do us. Their words of gratitude are a gift and should be received in the same manner they are given, freely and without strings attached.

Whenever we find ourselves expecting recognition for our parenting efforts, we're on a slippery slope that inevitably leads to feeling resentment toward our children when we don't get it. By expecting them to notice and acknowledge our efforts, we're covertly hoping they'll make us feel seen, valued, and appreciated. This is not only an unfair expectation to put on a young child, it's also unreasonable. They lack the context to recognize how much we do for them, because they have nothing to compare it to. More important, their brains are still developing, so they don't yet consider the needs or feelings of another at the very same time as they are experiencing their own. They don't understand the enormity of our efforts or the extent of the sacrifices we make for them simply because it doesn't occur to them!

Despite children's apparent lack of appreciation, we should consistently show them ours. By being on the receiving end of our heartfelt thanks they'll come to know how being thanked makes them feel, and someday they'll be moved to freely give appreciation to you and others. More than that, by releasing the expectation that our children will show gratitude for our effort and sacrifices, we'll be inwardly claiming our role as their unconditional caregivers who do what we do out of love rather than for recognition. There is infinite fulfillment of a loving parent's heart to be found in that.

Here's what you can do...

Remembering that your young child is immature rather than ungrateful will release you from trying to extract appreciation out of them. While you should certainly show your gratitude when they or others do things for you, don't expect that this will result in them expressing their appreciation of you just yet. With maturity and life experience they will begin to comprehend that you went above and beyond for them and when this sinks in, the appreciation that comes your way will be genuine, heartfelt, and freely given.

Today's parenting affirmation: I will freely express my gratitude in the presence of my child.

53. Please Don't Worry So Much About Me

．．．．．．．．．．．．．．．．．．．．．．．．．．．．

PARENTS ARE often perplexed when I suggest they not worry so much about their children. While worrying is natural for most people, this doesn't mean it's helpful. For many parents, perpetual worrying has been unquestionably accepted as an integral part of the parenting deal, but it doesn't have to be.

My first few years of parenting were largely fuelled by worry and concern for the well-being of my children. It's what kept me up at night and eventually led me to doing the work I do now. Although that last part is a fulfilling outcome, my worry kept me from fully experiencing much of the joy that was right in front of me. For many years, I thought worrying was caring because they are so tightly intertwined. It took me a long while to unravel them and see that it is possible to care deeply without worrying incessantly. Not quite all of the time, but much of the time.

When caring feelings begin to tangle with feelings of worry, parenting becomes very stressful. We risk involuntarily becoming consumed by our distress, and our caring feelings may unconsciously be eclipsed by the extent of our worry. Parents' reactions are driven by the fear of what might happen if they fail their children in some way. Nonstop worry saps our joy and drains our energy like cellphone apps running in the background and depleting the battery.

Ironically, for some parents, worrying consistently provides them with a false sense of productivity and purpose. As long as they are worrying, they feel they're doing something, even though their anxious thoughts may not result in actively supporting children in the ways they need.

Once parents become conscious of how consumed they are by their worry, they begin to see how much valuable energy has been wasted on anticipating the worst and trying to predict and control the future. Changing our worry-fuelled ways starts with noticing when we're doing it. This awareness naturally leads us to start taking charge of our thoughts, and with time, we begin channelling our energy in more helpful and constructive ways.

All that said, a little bit of worry is not only healthy, it can also be very helpful. Just the right amount of concern doesn't overwhelm and can provide the impetus needed to motivate parents to seek insight, change their ways, and become the parents their children need them to be. It can also be the source of the inspiration needed to get exhausted parents to keep showing up for their children and not give up, even when they think they can't possibly go on. How much worry is just enough? Well, that depends on the individual. Each of us need to decide how much worry is helpful and how much is hurtful.

Here's what you can do...

Pay attention to your thoughts and try to notice how often you are mistaking incessant worrying for deep caring. When you are parenting from a place of fear you can't help but become controlling and prescriptive under the guise of caring, but your fear-driven actions may not be experienced by your child as loving or supportive. If you catch yourself worrying, try to redirect your focus on identifying the need that may be driving their concerning behaviour and put your energy toward meeting that.

If you are struggling with overwhelming feelings of worry or anxiety, consider seeking the support of a professional counsellor or therapist.

Today's parenting affirmation: I recognize that I do not have to worry in order to be caring.

54. I'm Still Growing and So Are You

. . . .

ALTHOUGH I consider myself to be a patient person, I've certainly had parenting moments where my tolerance has been tested and I've failed dismally. One occasion that stands out in my memory is the rainy day I took my young daughter on a field trip to the pumpkin patch and I lost all patience. The day started out full of excitement and enthusiasm, but after trudging through a muddy field for hours and lugging a heavy pumpkin that had taken far too long to select, things started to unravel. We were both exhausted and frustrated. We should have left much earlier, but we didn't, and trailing a wailing, overstimulated child to the exit in full view of gaping parents and teachers took its toll on me.

By the time we reached the car my head was pounding, my heart was racing, and my palms were sweating. I was so embarrassed. All that was needed was to get my daughter buckled into the car seat so that we could leave and end the nightmare. Unfortunately, it wasn't that simple. Her resistance increased and resulted in her arching her back and kicking her legs, making securing her into her seat almost impossible. After a few minutes of struggle and deft manoeuvring, I got it done and then hurriedly drove off with the sound of my heart pumping loudly in my ears. I don't ever remember having felt this stirred up before and it scared me.

My sweet child was raging in the back seat. Furious with what had just happened and not able to let it go, she began kicking the back of my seat and with each thud I felt my jaw clenching tighter. I spoke in a controlled but stern way insisting that she stop what she was doing right now. Of course she didn't. She was a four-year-old who was exhausted, having just endured a marathon session of pumpkin-picking in the pouring rain. I was blind to considering this crucial context when I needed it most.

The next thing I knew, I had pulled the car over and was standing at her car door asking if she wanted to get out and live at this stranger's house because I couldn't take it anymore. I was so overwhelmed I had lost all perspective of what was really going on. I was the one behaving as if I were the victim when clearly, I wasn't. I was holding her responsible for my immature behaviour and, in doing so, had stooped to doing something I had never imagined I'd be capable of: threatening to give her away because of her appropriately immature behaviour. That moment haunts me to this day, but it was pivotal in helping me to see that even the most caring, well-intentioned people may have inside of them a level of frustration they might never have encountered prior to having their own children.

Adjusting to the role of being an adult responsible for the well-being of young children is a process. It's one we're meant to grow into and we're fuelled to do so by the love we have for our children. One of the greatest unexpected by-products of raising children is the opportunity to grow into the people we're capable of being. Not every adult is open to this invitation and those who resist miss out on much of the joy and personal growth to be found amidst the chaos and frustration of everyday life with young children.

Up until we take on the responsibility of caring for children, we have relative freedom with respect to how we manage much of our lives. For the most part, we're in control of when we sleep and when we wake, where we choose to go, and how we manage our time. As any parent knows, much of our ability to choose what happens and when, disappears once we become parents. Although we anticipate it, we still need to adapt to it because unless we do, we risk becoming frustrated, resentful people who cling to what once was, instead of accepting the gift of what now is.

Each day parents are presented with numerous opportunities disguised as challenges. If we're willing to see these emotionally charged interactions as gateways to our own development, these moments can empower us to show up for our children, and also for ourselves. Without their presence we'd likely spend our days avoiding our own expansion. When we see our children as having come to us for a greater purpose, the deep love we have for them leads us to the previously unattended parts of ourselves and in so doing we begin to feel more whole. We wouldn't likely willingly venture here by ourselves, but we can courageously show up and do it with them.

Here's what you can do...

When you find yourself feeling provoked by your child, rather than putting all your focus on what it is they appear to be doing to upset you, give some of your valuable attention to the emotion being stirred up inside of you. Although you'll likely still feel strongly that you're struggling against your child's behaviour, you'll begin to see that you're also being invited to take a look at the parts of yourself you can still grow because it's never too late. Our children are here to support our growth and development just as much, and perhaps even more, than we're here to do this for them.

Today's parenting affirmation: I recognize and appreciate the opportunity to continue my growth alongside my child.

55. I Don't Need a Perfect Parent

THERE'S SOMETHING about wanting to be the best parent possible that leads us to think we need to be perfect to be worthy of raising the children who have been entrusted to us. While it's a noble idea, it's an inherently flawed premise because there's no such thing as a perfect parent. No matter how hard we try or how desperately we want to be perfect, it just won't happen because we're human. Most of us already know this, but some of us still struggle to let go of the idea of parenting perfection because we can sense the potential within us to become more of who we're capable of being.

I consider the longing for perfection to be a form of soul suffering. By repeatedly reminding ourselves we're not yet living up to our ideals, we're feeding our feelings of incompetence and unworthiness. We're also unconsciously talking ourselves down from becoming the parents we want to be. If you're anything like me, you probably focus more attention on what you're *not* doing than all that you're *already* doing. Our desire for perfection morphs into constant reminders of how far we have yet to go. Rather than inspiring us to keep going, these thoughts may become self-admonishments that repeatedly play in our heads and become beliefs about our perceived incompetence. Without an awareness of what's unconsciously happening, we may begin to buy into these beliefs of unworthiness and parenting imperfection.

Letting go of the goal of perfection isn't an excuse for not trying to be a better parent than you currently are.

What it does is free you from the tormenting voice that wears you down and makes you feel as though you're consistently failing to meet the idealistic goals you've been imagining. By getting clear on what you want to do differently or do better, you'll find yourself setting boundaries on the expansive ideals you've been holding on to. Releasing the notion of being perfect isn't about giving up your aspirations. It's about fine-tuning them so you can develop clear intentions and get on with the job of showing up for your children in all your imperfection rather than wasting your energy thinking about how you're not the perfect parent.

There's no time like the present to start paying closer attention to your real or perceived shortcomings. You've no doubt heard the phrase: "You have to name it to claim it." To that insight I'd like to add a deeper layer suggesting, "You have to feel it in order to deal with it." If you're lacking patience, be open enough to lament its absence. If you tend to dump your frustration onto your children, be courageous enough to own it. If you're crippled by parental guilt for what you've done or haven't done, be vulnerable enough to sit with it. Whatever it is you're feeling, you'll need to become conscious of it because that's at the core of what's holding you back from becoming the parent you want to be for your children and the person you long to be for yourself.

Here's what you can do...

Give up the idea that you'll ever be a perfect parent, but don't ever give up trying to be the best parent you can be. By being willing to consistently show up for your children and to feel your human imperfection, you'll be more open to seeing what you can do differently, and you won't give up on them or yourself. Always remember your children don't need a perfect parent; they need a real one who loves them like you do.

Today's parenting affirmation: I will never give up trying to become the parent my child needs, or the person I want to become.

Mantra for Parents

What other people think of me or
of my child is none of my business,

My responsibility is to
myself and to my child,

And to the relationship we share.

Everything else is outside of that.

(Repeat daily or as often as needed.)

Additional Reading

OR READERS SEEKING deeper insight into the developmental processes required for maturation, the following information has been reprinted with the permission of Deborah MacNamara, from her book *Rest, Play, Grow: Making Sense of Preschoolers (Or Anyone Who Acts Like One)* (Vancouver: Aona Books, 2016).

How Young Children Mature:
Emergent, Adaptive, and Integrative Processes

What are the inner grown processes that drive a child to become a socially and emotionally responsible individual?

Based on decades of distilling developmental research, theory, and practice to the essence, Gordon Neufeld has put the pieces together to form a coherent theory of human maturation. Growth is driven by three distinct inner processes, which are spontaneous in development, but not inevitable:

1. The emergent process gives rise to the capacity to function as a *separate person* and to develop a strong sense of agency.

2. The adaptive process enables a person to *adapt* to life circumstances and overcome adversity.

3. The integrative process helps a child grow into a *social being* with the capacity to engage in relationships without compromising personal integrity and identity.

The presence or absence of the emergent, adaptive, and integrative processes are the measurements or "vital signs" we can use to assess the developmental trajectory of a child and their overall maturity. It is our human potential to become *separate, adaptive, and social beings*, but this can only be realized when adults play a supportive role in cultivating the conditions for growth.

From Gordon Neufeld, "Synthesis of the Unfolding of Human Potential," Neufeld Intensive I: Making Sense of Kids course (Vancouver: Neufeld Institute, 2013). Reprinted with permission.

Emergent process

The first goal of healthy development is viability as a *separate being* and involves gradual movement from dependence, to independence, to adult autonomy through the *emergent process*. The emergent process thrusts a child toward selfhood and exploring their world. Play is the natural sphere in which children first start to express this emergent self. Play is the birthplace of growth into personhood, but only occurs when children are at rest in relationships with caring adults.

The emergent process bears many fruits, including a capacity to function when separate from one's attachments, as well as to form interests and goals. Emergent children exude a wonderful vitality and are rarely bored. There is vibrancy to life, a sense of wonder, and a curiosity that leads to experimentation, imagining, and daydreaming. It is through this emergent process that imaginary friends are born.

Emergent children are also known for their venturing-forth spirit that drives them to be enthusiastic learners as they strive to make sense of the world. They actively shape and assume responsibility for their life story instead of becoming a character in someone else's. There is such a strong desire to be a unique being that plagiarizing, copying, or imitating are rejected as affronts to the integrity of selfhood. The anthem of an emergent child is "Me-do" or "I do it myself."

Adaptive process

The second maturation process that underlies human potential is the *adaptive process*. It is at the root of how we become resilient, resourceful, and able to recover from adversity. You cannot teach a child to become adaptive and this process is not realized without the right conditions being present. The adaptive process helps equip children with the resilience to handle what lies ahead and thrive despite obstacles. It enables children to learn from mistakes, benefit from correction, and engage in trial and error. The adaptive process underlies our capacity to transform when up against things in our world we cannot change.

The adaptive process is also the answer to dealing with tantrums and aggression in young children. They are routinely upset when their agendas are thwarted, unleashing frustration and attempts to negotiate a better outcome. They are not born preprogrammed with a set of limits and restrictions that prepare them for everyday life. They sometimes look at us in amazement as if to say, "Why can't I have another cookie? What kind of place is this?"

Young children are driven to possess, be first, and get what they want because of their egocentric nature. The adaptive process helps them relinquish their agendas and realize they can survive when things don't go their way. One of the fastest ways to create an "entitled" or "spoiled" child is by circumventing the adaptive process and preventing feelings of upset from occurring about all the things they cannot change. The character Veruca Salt in *Charlie and the Chocolate Factory* is the epitome of such a child. She orders her parents around continuously, "I want it, and I want it now, Daddy!" The parents live in fear of her eruptions and busy themselves constantly meeting her demands. A parent's job is to help prepare a child to live in the world as it exists, with the upsets and disappointments that are part of it.

Integration process

The third maturation process that grows a child is integration. This process is responsible for transforming children into social beings who are mature and responsible. The integrative process requires brain development and emotional maturity. The Swiss developmental psychologist Jean Piaget called it the "5- to 7-year shift," when a child comes to appreciate context and take into account more than one perspective at a time. As this shift occurs, young children will become increasingly tempered in their expression of thoughts and feelings. They will start to exhibit impulse control in the face of strong emotions. Instead of lashing out, they might say, "I half-hate you right now!" and "I want to hit you!" but they do not. They will exhibit patience, despite frustration at having to wait. They will be capable of sharing from a place of true consideration and not because they are told to do so. They will be able to persist toward a goal without collapsing in frustration. A civilized form will slowly appear and naturally diminish the immature ways of relating known as "the preschooler personality."

One of the most important developmental resolutions of the integrative process is the capacity to be a separate self in the midst of so many other people. When you are able to hold on to your own point of view while considering another person's experiences, it provides greater breadth and depth in perspective. Young children can only operate out of one perspective at a time and it is usually expressed as, "It's mine." A mature person should be able to disagree with someone while preserving a sense of togetherness. "I can see your point of view—would you like to hear mine?" Integration should also give rise to a separate self that doesn't succumb to peer pressure, blending, cloning, or fusing. As Katie, a seven-year-old girl, said to her friend while playing, "I don't want to be your pet baby rabbit. I don't like rabbits. I want to be the hamster mother instead."

Our ultimate destiny as social beings is to fully participate in our communities and possess a level of moral reasoning that goes beyond the "I" and considers the needs of the whole. If we want our children to participate as global citizens and become stewards of the earth, they need to become mature social beings. Our potential as social beings is unlocked through healthy parent/child relationships.

There is an organic solution to the immaturity of young children. There is a natural, developmental process and parents play a critical role in it. When the conditions for growth have been assured, the inner emergent, adaptive, and integration processes will launch a child's trajectory toward personhood. A failure to mature is also part of the human condition, but this is where adults must be a child's best bet. Selfhood cannot be taught or forced; it must be nurtured, cultivated, preserved, and protected.

Recommended Resources

THE DEVELOPMENTAL-RELATIONAL APPROACH of Gordon Neufeld resonates deeply with me and some of the themes in this book are rooted in his approach to making sense of children. Although I have only lightly touched on some aspects of development and attachment, for anyone seeking a deeper understanding of the Neufeld paradigm, I recommend that you explore the following resources.

The Neufeld Institute

The Neufeld Institute is committed to putting parents back into the driver's seat with regard to their own children. Our mission is to use developmental science to rejoin parents and teachers to their own natural intuition. All our endeavours are based on the understanding that the context for raising children is their attachment to those responsible for them.

The Neufeld Institute is headquartered in Vancouver, Canada, and uses the latest technology to provide training and education throughout the world. Neufeld faculty and Neufeld course facilitators are currently practising in ten countries: Canada, the United States, Mexico, Germany, Israel, Finland, Sweden, Denmark, Australia, and New Zealand.

The Neufeld Institute offers an insight-based parent education program through online and on-site courses and presentations, as well as a continuing education program for parents, educators, and professionals. Training programs exist for those wishing to facilitate Neufeld Institute courses, as well as for helping professionals seeking to practise this approach through parent consulting.

Our online campus supports the growing number of those who are teaching and practising the paradigm throughout the world. This campus is accessible to individuals in five languages and serves to join the sparks that are happening in diverse settlings around the globe.

The Neufeld Institute is incorporated as a not-for-profit society in British Columbia and registered as a charitable organization in Canada.

Neufeld Institute Courses

The following online courses are available to anyone wanting to dive deeper into the developmental and relational theory I have touched upon in this book.

Please visit www.neufeldinstitute.org for course outlines and registration information:

Neufeld Intensive Courses

Neufeld Intensive I: Making Sense of Kids
Neufeld Intensive II: The Separation Complex
Neufeld Intensive III: Becoming Attached
Advanced: Making Sense of Therapy

Power to Parent Series

The Vital Connection
Helping Children Grow Up
Common Challenges

Play Courses

Play 101
Play and Attachment
Play and Emotion
Preserving Play in the Digital World

Other Neufeld Institute Courses

The Attachment Puzzle
Making Sense of Adolescence
Making Sense of Preschoolers
Teachability Factor

The Science of Emotion
Transplanting Children
Alpha Children
Bullies: Their Making and Unmaking
Home Education: Rest, Play, Learn
Making Sense of Aggression
Making Sense of Anxiety
Making Sense of Attention Problems
Making Sense of Counterwill
Making Sense of Discipline
Making Sense of Hyperactivity
Making Sense of Resilience

Book Resources

MacNamara, Deborah. *Rest, Play, Grow: Making Sense of Preschoolers (Or Anyone Who Acts Like One)*. Vancouver: Aona Books, 2016.

Neufeld, Gordon, and Gabor Maté. *Hold On to Your Kids: Why Parents Need to Matter More Than Peers*. Toronto: Vintage Canada, 2013.

Gratitudes

EVERY PERSON I'VE crossed paths with, be it in person or in some other way, has played a part in the writing of this book. Although it's impossible to remember who did what, or said what, it has all contributed to what I share and for that, I am truly grateful.

My heartfelt appreciation goes to the following people who have touched my life indelibly:

My parents, Jack and Brenda Burchell, for all your love and for seeing the very best in me.

My siblings, Tony Burchell and Lisa Hartdegen, for all the ways in which you show up for your families. You inspire me.

My Oupa-Darling, Herbert Ellis, who stoked my love of learning and the meaning of words, and my granny, Louise Ellis, who told me to always listen to my heart.

My Sotho Gogo (African grandma), Lizzie Mariti, who loved me, helped care for me, and made me want to become a teacher.

My parents-in-law, Gavin Snr and Joan Miller, for the love and support you generously give our family.

My teaching partners, Patty Lees and Carol Carrick, for showing me how to lean into my calling as a teacher, and Sheila Verner for allowing us the space to do it in our own ways.

My friend and mentor Colleen Drobot, who gave a parent talk one rainy night and set me on a new trajectory. Your presence, insight, and willingness to share from your heart has played a pivotal part in what I share in this book.

My advisor, the late Gail Carney, for sitting with me on a bench in Vanier Park and suggesting I apply to the Neufeld Institute to join the facilitators program. I'll always remember the glint in her eye and her chuckle when I told her that I didn't imagine myself ever being comfortable with public speaking.

My Neufeld Institute family:

Gordon Neufeld, for generously sharing your wisdom and stirring in me the need to contribute what I've learned in ways that feel authentic.

Joy Neufeld, for the pearls of personal insight you've given me over the years and for filling me up, both literally and figuratively, when I'm in your presence.

The Neufeld faculty and fellow students, for the added depth of insight and warmth you bring to the campus experience.

Jane Irvin, for seeing a path ahead of me when I couldn't yet see it for myself.

My lovely friend Tina Esposito, for creating my very first website and course posters.

My local ladies Wendy Krill, Bernadette Pittini, Lauren Hilliard, Michelle Blane, Janine Grant, Linda Marzec,

Michelle Head, and Laila Abulhusn for your thought-provoking questions and for consistently showing up when I first began offering parent groups.

My soul sister Deborah MacNamara, for inviting me to become your sidekick in various settings and for deepening my understanding along the way. I so appreciate the good times and laughs we've shared. Having you write the foreword to this book means the world to me.

My dear friend and confidante Judith de Niet, for gently guiding me to see things differently and empowering me to live my life fully so that my dreams get checked off my to-do list. A special thanks to your girls, Penelope and Eady, for innocently confirming the title of this book.

My yoginis Anthea Hughes and Anna Oldfield, for generously holding space so I could gain strength and clarity on my mat and take it with me into the world. I feel blessed to call you friends.

My dear Pam Leo, for being ahead of your time and for laying the connection parenting foundation upon which the rest of us walk.

My faraway friends Becky Eanes, Lelia Schott, and Kirsty Lee, for your friendship and support and for helping me to see that what I have to say can make a positive difference in the lives of others when it's shared.

My forever friend Anne Uebbing, for our long walks and talks, and for your unwavering belief in what I have to offer. Thank you for helping me in myriad ways.

My Page Two team: Trena White, for listening to my ideas and getting behind this book wholeheartedly from the get-go; Gabrielle Narsted, for driving the bus and making sure we were all on it; Peter Cocking, Taysia Louie, and Prateeba Perumal, for taking my idea for a cover and turning it into something even better than I could imagine; Jessica Werb, for introducing me to the world of publicity and helping me to get it done; Shannon Whibbs, for waving your copy-editing wand over my manuscript; Alison Strobel, for making sure that every word, dot, and dash is exactly as it needs to be; Lorraine Toor, for all your help getting this book into the hands of readers around the world; the people behind the scenes I've yet to meet, thank you for your part in making this book a reality.

My editor extraordinaire, Barbara Johnston, for your skilled guidance and ability to make me feel even more excited about our project with each conversation. Thank you for your thoughtful suggestions and for helping me to convey what I needed to say more clearly and succinctly.

My husband, Gavin, for being by my side. Your loving presence and unwavering support have made it possible for me to spend time with our girls as they've grown up, and for that I'll be forever grateful. I couldn't have wished for a more kind and loving husband, or a more caring father to our children. I love you, my dear.

And lastly, my lovely girls, Caite and Erin, for being who you are and for inspiring me to never stop trying to be the parent and person I long to be. I love you both with all my heart.

About
the Author

BRIDGETT MILLER IS a preschool and elementary teacher, remedial therapist, presenter, and parent consultant. She is an Authorized Facilitator of the Neufeld Institute and the creator of the popular Look with Love and Parenting with Intention conscious parenting pages on Facebook and Instagram. Bridgett supports adults in nurturing the children in their lives using their heads and their hearts, drawing on her almost two decades of personal experience as a teacher and parent. Born and raised in South Africa, she now resides with her husband and two daughters in Vancouver, Canada. Some of Bridgett's favourite pastimes include writing, reading, creating, gardening, yoga, meditation, and listening to audiobooks and podcasts. She's at her happiest when she's spending time with her family, hiking in the forest, digging in the garden, walking her dogs, travelling the world—and, of course, interacting with people like you. Please visit www.bridgettmiller.com to contact Bridgett, join her email list, or send her a note.

CPSIA information can be obtained
at www.ICGtesting.com
Printed in the USA
LVHW042152290420
654638LV00005B/322

9 781777 064907